WITHDRAWN

HUMAN NATURE

OPPOSING VIEWPOINTS®

OTHER BOOKS OF RELATED INTEREST

OPPOSING VIEWPOINTS SERIES

America Beyond 2001
American Values
America's Future
Biomedical Ethics
Civil Liberties
Constructing a Life Philosophy
Culture Wars
Death & Dying
Human Rights
Suicide
Sexual Values
War

CURRENT CONTROVERSIES SERIES

Ethics
Nationalism and Ethnic Conflict
Politicians and Ethics

AT ISSUE SERIES

Anti-Semitism
Business Ethics
The Ethics of Euthanasia
Physician-Assisted Suicide

HUMAN NATURE

OPPOSING VIEWPOINTS®

Mark Ray Schmidt, Associate Professor of English,
University of Arkansas at Monticello, Book Editor

David L. Bender, Publisher
Bruno Leone, Executive Editor
Bonnie Szumski, Editorial Director
David M. Haugen, Managing Editor

OPPOSING
VIEWPOINTS®
SERIES

Greenhaven Press, Inc., San Diego, California

BD
450
.H858
1999

Cover photo: Image Club

Library of Congress Cataloging-in-Publication Data

Human nature : opposing viewpoints / Mark Ray Schmidt, book editor.
    p.   cm. — (Opposing viewpoints series)
    Includes bibliographical references and index.
    ISBN 0-7377-0073-4 (lib. : alk. paper). —
ISBN 0-7377-0072-6 (pbk. : alk. paper)
    1. Philosophical anthropology. I. Schmidt, Mark Ray, 1953–   .
II. Series.
BD450.H858 1999
128—dc21   98-31859
                                                                    CIP

Greenhaven Press, Inc., P.O. Box 289009
San Diego, CA 92198-9009

"CONGRESS SHALL MAKE NO LAW...ABRIDGING THE FREEDOM OF SPEECH, OR OF THE PRESS."

First Amendment to the U.S. Constitution

The basic foundation of our democracy is the First Amendment guarantee of freedom of expression. The Opposing Viewpoints Series is dedicated to the concept of this basic freedom and the idea that it is more important to practice it than to enshrine it.

CONTENTS

WHY CONSIDER OPPOSING VIEWPOINTS?

"The only way in which a human being can make some approach to knowing the whole of a subject is by hearing what can be said about it by persons of every variety of opinion and studying all modes in which it can be looked at by every character of mind. No wise man ever acquired his wisdom in any mode but this."

John Stuart Mill

In our media-intensive culture it is not difficult to find differing opinions. Thousands of newspapers and magazines and dozens of radio and television talk shows resound with differing points of view. The difficulty lies in deciding which opinion to agree with and which "experts" seem the most credible. The more inundated we become with differing opinions and claims, the more essential it is to hone critical reading and thinking skills to evaluate these ideas. Opposing Viewpoints books address this problem directly by presenting stimulating debates that can be used to enhance and teach these skills. The varied opinions contained in each book examine many different aspects of a single issue. While examining these conveniently edited opposing views, readers can develop critical thinking skills such as the ability to compare and contrast authors' credibility, facts, argumentation styles, use of persuasive techniques, and other stylistic tools. In short, the Opposing Viewpoints Series is an ideal way to attain the higher-level thinking and reading skills so essential in a culture of diverse and contradictory opinions.

In addition to providing a tool for critical thinking, Opposing Viewpoints books challenge readers to question their own strongly held opinions and assumptions. Most people form their opinions on the basis of upbringing, peer pressure, and personal, cultural, or professional bias. By reading carefully balanced opposing views, readers must directly confront new ideas as well as the opinions of those with whom they disagree. This is not to simplistically argue that everyone who reads opposing views will—or should—change his or her opinion. Instead, the series enhances readers' understanding of their own views by encouraging confrontation with opposing ideas. Careful examination of others' views can lead to the readers' understanding of the logical inconsistencies in their own opinions, perspective on why they hold an opinion, and the consideration of the possibility that their opinion requires further evaluation.

EVALUATING OTHER OPINIONS

To ensure that this type of examination occurs, Opposing Viewpoints books present all types of opinions. Prominent spokespeople on different sides of each issue as well as well-known professionals from many disciplines challenge the reader. An additional goal of the series is to provide a forum for other, less known, or even unpopular viewpoints. The opinion of an ordinary person who has had to make the decision to cut off life support from a terminally ill relative, for example, may be just as valuable and provide just as much insight as a medical ethicist's professional opinion. The editors have two additional purposes in including these less known views. One, the editors encourage readers to respect others' opinions—even when not enhanced by professional credibility. It is only by reading or listening to and objectively evaluating others' ideas that one can determine whether they are worthy of consideration. Two, the inclusion of such viewpoints encourages the important critical thinking skill of objectively evaluating an author's credentials and bias. This evaluation will illuminate an author's reasons for taking a particular stance on an issue and will aid in readers' evaluation of the author's ideas.

As series editors of the Opposing Viewpoints Series, it is our hope that these books will give readers a deeper understanding of the issues debated and an appreciation of the complexity of even seemingly simple issues when good and honest people disagree. This awareness is particularly important in a democratic society such as ours in which people enter into public debate to determine the common good. Those with whom one disagrees should not be regarded as enemies but rather as people whose views deserve careful examination and may shed light on one's own.

Thomas Jefferson once said that "difference of opinion leads to inquiry, and inquiry to truth." Jefferson, a broadly educated man, argued that "if a nation expects to be ignorant and free . . . it expects what never was and never will be." As individuals and as a nation, it is imperative that we consider the opinions of others and examine them with skill and discernment. The Opposing Viewpoints Series is intended to help readers achieve this goal.

David L. Bender & Bruno Leone,
Series Editors

Greenhaven Press anthologies primarily consist of previously published material taken from a variety of sources, including periodicals, books, scholarly journals, newspapers, government documents, and position papers from private and public organizations. These original sources are often edited for length and to ensure their accessibility for a young adult audience. The anthology editors also change the original titles of these works in order to clearly present the main thesis of each viewpoint and to explicitly indicate the opinion presented in the viewpoint. These alterations are made in consideration of both the reading and comprehension levels of a young adult audience. Every effort is made to ensure that Greenhaven Press accurately reflects the original intent of the authors included in this anthology.

INTRODUCTION

"In a time when change in certain aspects of 'human nature' has become necessary to the survival of our species, it is comforting to know that it can be done and has been done. The problem of the scientist is to find out how."
—Ralph Linton, The Study of Man, 1936

Coming to understand human nature is vitally important to everyone. Store managers need to appeal to the needs and desires of potential customers. Teachers need to understand how to motivate students to learn. Engineers need to design tractors, computers, and public transportation systems which are "user friendly." In every field of study and in every area of life, people are trying to understand why other people do what they do. Those people with the best understanding of basic human motivations, or human nature, are the most likely to succeed in their chosen field.

The study of human nature is also unavoidable. As people work, play, and study, they form general ideas about human nature. These ideas or assumptions usually go unnoticed until someone notices a startling event or bizarre behavior. Suddenly someone says, "That's weird! That's unnatural! Why did they act that way?" This response is caused by a conflict between what is assumed to be normal, natural behavior for humans and the particular event which violates that expectation. Without realizing it, we are constantly forming and refining our general beliefs about human nature. Such assumptions about humanity need to be brought to our attention and evaluated. Otherwise, we will be blinded by a prejudice.

Human Nature: Opposing Viewpoints offers a survey of some of the ways in which writers have sought to understand human nature. Many writers have found that the social environment of a person is the best way to understand humans. Early childhood training, traumatic experiences, peer pressure, economic pressures, and other factors come together to make people do what they do. Other writers have pointed out that genetic factors (aggressive instincts, sexual impulses, hunger, and social instincts) are the key to understanding human behavior. Still others have championed views of human nature based on human freedom, human rationality, or human spirituality. There have also been a number of thinkers who have doubted the existence of a nature common to all humans.

The subject of human nature is filled with controversy. Since so many people disagree about what constitutes human nature and how to understand it, some might be tempted to throw their hands up and declare the study of human nature a waste of time. Yet such a course of action would be impossible: studying human nature is essential to understanding ourselves and the world around us.

This collection of opposing viewpoints offers a broad cross-section of opinions on the contentious issue of human nature. The selections are drawn from a diverse group of authors representing an equally diverse group of disciplines: philosophy, psychology, biology, theology, natural history, literature, and more.

WHAT FACTORS INFLUENCE HUMAN NATURE?

CHAPTER PREFACE

A number of psychologists, sociologists, philosophers, and biologists have concluded that human nature is a composite of all the forces in a person's life. Because some experiences are similar for all humans (growing up, feeling helpless, learning new skills, and learning to compromise with others), humans typically have behavior patterns that are also similar. These similarities are summarized by the term human nature. However, human nature does not imply that all humans have exactly the same traits; some people have unique experiences and are thus exceptions to the rule. As psychiatrist Erich Fromm has suggested, humans are rather easy to understand and are somewhat predictable, particularly if one has insight into the conditions that have shaped the individual.

Yet on the other hand, many social and biological scientists have embraced the idea that human behavior is rooted in certain biological instincts. After years of carefully studying instinctive behavior in animals, zoologist Konrad Lorenz concluded that all of the basic behaviors of humans (aggression, love, religion, and social relationships) are rooted in and guided by our instincts. While acknowledging some social influences, this approach to human nature focuses on the underlying unity of all human behavior. Biologist Edward O. Wilson also promotes this perspective.

In opposition to these approaches is a third point of view. While acknowledging that social forces often influence human behavior and that genetic forces also play a role in human behavior, this third group of thinkers believes that individuals can rise above social and genetic influences. This ability to resist such influence is normally linked to a unique freedom found in each individual. Sometimes this freedom is associated with rationality and sometimes it is associated with spirituality, which transcends the limitations of our physical existence. Although this approach contains a number of conflicting positions, it is unified by a belief that humans are not controlled by either genetics or social forces. George W. Morgan represents this perspective. Morgan explains that humans are free and complex, and he rejects defining human nature in terms of heredity or environment, asserting that humans are free to either accept or resist those forces. Furthermore, Morgan maintains that humans are too mysterious and complicated to be fully understood.

Morgan finds that human nature is difficult to define, yet he is confident that human nature is something real. In contrast, writer and philosopher Jean-Paul Sartre rejects the idea of human nature. While Sartre agrees with Morgan that humans are free, Sartre is much more extreme in his understanding of freedom. He feels that humans can freely reject any influence, whether genetic or social. Sartre rejects the idea of human nature because he does not see any limitation on human thought or behavior. While admitting that people are often predictable in their actions, Sartre believes that people are always free to reject their past patterns of behavior and to create new lives for themselves. Therefore, freedom, according to Sartre, has no limitations.

Sartre is not alone in rejecting the concept of human nature. A number of twentieth-century writers, including the psychologist B.F. Skinner, have strongly rejected any notion of human nature. Often these people, in contrast to Sartre, focus on the ways that humans are shaped by their family background, social context, and economic situation.

Mortimer J. Adler opposes these critics and argues that it is necessary to accept the idea of human nature. Adler agrees that humans in different cultures are different from each other and that people are greatly influenced by the social and linguistic forces surrounding them. However, Adler defends the idea of human nature by pointing to the underlying common "potentialities" found in every human. For example, Adler admits that children in England learn to speak English and children in Spain learn to speak Spanish; yet despite these obvious social influences, Adler points to the fact that all humans (except for those with unique physical impairments) learn to speak some language. The use of some language is only one of the "potentialities" that Adler sees in humans. Morals, social relationships, and rational thought processes are some of the other features that Adler finds common in all humans. Adler further develops his argument, concluding that humans have a limited amount of freedom to accept or reject the social influences that surround them.

While reading the selections in the following chapters the reader should note the various ways the authors have used this term. If human nature exists, the reader should also consider whether such a nature originates from a social, biological, rational, spiritual context, or a combination of these factors.

| "The most beautiful as well as the most ugly inclinations of man are not part of a fixed and biologically given human nature, but result from the social process which creates man."

HUMAN NATURE IS SHAPED BY SOCIETY

Erich Fromm

Erich Fromm (1900–1980) was trained in both sociology and psychoanalysis. He was born in Germany, but moved to the United States in the 1930s. He wrote many popular books on the social and psychological forces which shape our lives. In *Escape from Freedom*, Fromm explains that people often experience social/political freedom as a burden which they try to avoid. His book is particularly concerned with the fact that many people in the 1930s were willing to submit to authoritarian governments in Italy, Germany, Russia, and other areas. This submission was a disappointment to many thinkers who believed that it is the nature of humans to seek freedom. In this context, Fromm explains that human nature is changeable. While admitting certain common physical and emotional needs in all humans, Fromm views human nature as molded by the social environment.

As you read, consider the following questions:

1. According to Fromm, how has human nature changed over the years?
2. What does Fromm mean by "dynamic adaption"?
3. Fromm states that human nature is not "infinitely malleable." What does he mean?

Reprinted by permission of Henry Holt and Company, Inc., from *Escape from Freedom*, by Erich Fromm. Copyright ©1941, 1969 by Erich Fromm.

The most beautiful as well as the most ugly inclinations of man are not part of a fixed and biologically given human nature, but result from the social process which creates man. In other words, society has not only a suppressing function—although it has that too—but it has also a creative function. Man's nature, his passions, and anxieties are a cultural product; as a matter of fact, man himself is the most important creation and achievement of the continuous human effort, the record of which we call history.

Humans Have Changed in History

It is the very task of social psychology to understand this process of man's creation in history. Why do certain definite changes of man's character take place from one historical epoch to another? Why is the spirit of the Renaissance different from that of the Middle Ages? Why is the character structure of man in monopolistic capitalism different from that in the nineteenth century? Social psychology has to explain why new abilities and new passions, bad or good, come into existence. Thus we find, for instance, that from the Renaissance up until our day men have been filled with a burning ambition for fame, while this striving which today seems so natural was little present in man of the medieval society. In the same period men developed a sense for the beauty of nature which they did not possess before. Again, in the Northern European countries, from the sixteenth century on, man developed an obsessional craving to work which had been lacking in a free man before that period.

But man is not only made by history—history is made by man. The solution of this seeming contradiction constitutes the field of social psychology. Its task is to show not only how passions, desires, anxieties change and develop as a result of the social process, but also how man's energies thus shaped into specific forms in their turn become productive forces, molding the social process. . . .

No Fixed Human Nature

Though there is no fixed human nature, we cannot regard human nature as being infinitely malleable and able to adapt itself to any kind of conditions without developing a psychological dynamism of its own. Human nature, though being the product of historical evolution, has certain inherent mechanisms and laws, to discover which is the task of psychology.

At this point it seems necessary for the full understanding of what has been said so far and also of what follows to discuss the notion of *adaptation*. This discussion offers at the same time an illustration of what we mean by psychological mechanisms and laws.

It seems useful to differentiate between "static" and "dynamic" adaptation. By static adaptation we mean such an adaptation to patterns as leaves the whole character structure unchanged and implies only the adoption of a new habit. An example of this kind of adaptation is the change from the Chinese habit of eating to the Western habit of using fork and knife. A Chinese coming to America will adapt himself to this new pattern, but this adaptation in itself has little effect on his personality; it does not arouse new drives or character traits.

HUMANS ADAPT TO ENVIRONMENT

By dynamic adaptation we refer to the kind of adaptation that occurs, for example, when a boy submits to the commands of his strict and threatening father—being too much afraid of him to do otherwise—and becomes a "good" boy. While he adapts himself to the necessities of the situation, something happens in him. He may develop an intense hostility against his father, which he represses, since it would be too dangerous to express it or even to be aware of it. This repressed hostility, however, though not manifest, is a dynamic factor in his character structure. It may create new anxiety and thus lead to still deeper submission; it may set up a vague defiance, directed against no one in particular but rather toward life in general. While here, too, as in the first case, an individual adapts himself to certain external circumstances, this kind of adaptation creates something new in him, arouses new drives and new anxieties. Every neurosis is an example of this dynamic adaptation; it is essentially an adaptation to such external conditions (particularly those of early childhood) as are in themselves irrational and, generally speaking, unfavorable to the growth and development of the child. Similarly, such socio-psychological phenomena as are comparable to neurotic phenomena (why they should not be called neurotic will be discussed later), like the presence of strong destructive or sadistic impulses in social groups, offer an example of dynamic adaptation to social conditions that are irrational and harmful to the development of men.

Besides the question of what kind of adaptation occurs, other questions need to be answered: What is it that forces man to adapt himself to almost any conceivable condition of life, and what are the limits of his adaptability?

In answering these questions the first phenomenon we have to discuss is the fact that there are certain sectors in man's nature that are more flexible and adaptable than others. Those strivings and character traits by which men differ from each other show a great amount of elasticity and malleability: love, destructiveness, sadism, the tendency to submit, the lust for power, detachment, the desire for self-aggrandizement, the passion for thrift, the enjoyment of sensual pleasure, and the fear of sensuality. These and many other strivings and fears to be found in man develop as a reaction to certain life conditions. They are not particularly flexible, for once they have become part of a person's character, they do not easily disappear or change into some other drive. But they are flexible in the sense that individuals, particularly in their childhood, develop the one or other need according to the whole mode of life they find themselves in. None of these needs is fixed and rigid as if it were an innate part of human nature which develops and has to be satisfied under all circumstances.

PHYSICAL NEEDS OF HUMANS

In contrast to those needs, there are others which are an indispensable part of human nature and imperatively need satisfaction, namely, those needs that are rooted in the physiological organization of man, like hunger, thirst, the need for sleep, and so on. For each of those needs there exists a certain threshold beyond which lack of satisfaction is unbearable, and when this threshold is transcended the tendency to satisfy the need assumes the quality of an all-powerful striving. All these physiologically conditioned needs can be summarized in the notion of a need for self-preservation. This need for self-preservation is that part of human nature which needs satisfaction under all circumstances and therefore forms the primary motive of human behavior.

To put this in a simple formula: man must eat, drink, sleep, protect himself against enemies, and so forth. In order to do all this he must work and produce. "Work," however, is nothing general or abstract. Work is always concrete work, that is, a specific kind of work in a specific kind of economic system. A person may work as a slave in a feudal system, as a peasant in an Indian pueblo, as an independent businessman in capitalistic society, as a salesgirl in a modern department store, as a worker on the endless belt of a big factory. These different kinds of work require entirely different personality traits and make for different kinds of relatedness to others. When man is born, the stage is set for him. He has to eat and drink, and therefore he has to work; and this means he has to work under the particular conditions and in the ways that are determined for him by the kind of society into which he is born. Both factors, his need to live and the social system, in principle are unalterable by him as an individual, and they are the factors which determine the development of those other traits that show greater plasticity.

CULTURAL PATTERNS GUIDE HUMANITY

Man, as Aristotle remarked, is a *social* animal. This fact introduces him into situations and originates problems and ways of solving them that have no precedent upon the organic biological level. For man is social in another sense than the bee and ant, since his activities are encompassed in an environment that is culturally transmitted, so that what man does and how he acts is determined not by organic structure and physical heredity alone but by the influence of cultural heredity, embedded in traditions, institutions, customs, and the purposes and beliefs they both carry and inspire.

John Dewey, *Logic*, 1938.

Thus the mode of life, as it is determined for the individual by the peculiarity of an economic system, becomes the primary factor in determining his whole character structure, because the imperative need for self-preservation forces him to accept the conditions under which he has to live. This does not mean that he cannot try, together with others, to effect certain economic and political changes; but primarily his personality is molded by the particular mode of life, as he has already been confronted with it as a child through the medium of the family, which represents all the features that are typical of a particular society or class.

THE NEED FOR COMMUNITY

The physiologically conditioned needs are not the only imperative part of man's nature. There is another part just as compelling, one which is not rooted in bodily processes but in the very essence of the human mode and practice of life: the need to be related to the world outside oneself, the need to avoid aloneness. To feel completely alone and isolated leads to mental disintegration just as physical starvation leads to death. This relatedness to others is not identical with physical contact. An individual may be alone in a physical sense for many years and yet he may be related to ideas, values, or at least social patterns that give him a feeling of communion and "belonging." On the other hand, he may live among people and yet be overcome with an utter feeling of isolation, the outcome of which, if it transcends a certain limit, is the state of insanity which schizophrenic disturbances represent. This lack of relatedness to values, symbols, patterns, we may call moral aloneness and state that moral aloneness is as intolerable as the physical aloneness. . . .

Human nature is neither a biologically fixed and innate sum total of drives nor is it a lifeless shadow of cultural patterns to which it adapts itself smoothly; it is the product of human evolution, but it also has certain inherent mechanisms and laws. There are certain factors in man's nature which are fixed and unchangeable: the necessity to satisfy the physiologically conditioned drives and the necessity to avoid isolation and moral aloneness. We have seen that the individual has to accept the mode of life rooted in the system of production and distribution peculiar for any given society. In the process of dynamic adaptation to culture, a number of powerful drives develop which motivate the actions and feelings of the individual. The individual may or may not be conscious of these drives, but in any case they are forceful and demand satisfaction once they have developed.

"Human nature is a hodgepodge of special genetic adaptations to an environment largely vanished, the world of the Ice-Age hunter-gatherer."

HUMAN NATURE IS SHAPED BY GENETICS

Edward O. Wilson

Edward O. Wilson has written several popular books to promote the new field of sociobiology, a blend of biology and sociology that uses principles from Darwin's theory of evolution. Wilson brings to Darwin's work a wealth of recent discoveries about animal behavior to help us understand human behavior. He is particularly concerned with those instinctive social behaviors of mammals, fish, and insects that have bearing on the instinctive social patterns of human life. Wilson believes that an understanding of the biology behind human action is essential to understanding humans. Wilson explains that morals, religion, and political beliefs are shaped and guided by our genes.

As you read, consider the following questions:

1. How does Wilson's assertion that human thoughts and actions are determined by genetics first developed in the Ice-Age influence his opinion of the future of humanity?
2. Why does Wilson believe that religion and morals are rooted in genetics?
3. Why does Wilson believe that humans need to develop a scientific evolutionary myth?

Reprinted by permission of the publisher from *On Human Nature*, by Edward O. Wilson. Cambridge, MA: Harvard University Press. Copyright ©1978 by the President and Fellows of Harvard College.

The intellectual solution of the first dilemma can be achieved by a deeper and more courageous examination of human nature that combines the findings of biology with those of the social sciences. The mind will be more precisely explained as an epiphenomenon of the neuronal machinery of the brain. That machinery is in turn the product of genetic evolution by natural selection acting on human populations for hundreds of thousands of years in their ancient environments. By a judicious extension of the methods and ideas of neurobiology, ethology, and sociobiology a proper foundation can be laid for the social sciences, and the discontinuity still separating the natural sciences on the one side and the social sciences and humanities on the other might be erased.

Moral Dilemmas

If this solution to the first dilemma proves even partially correct, it will lead directly to the second dilemma: the conscious choices that must be made among our innate mental propensities. The elements of human nature are the learning rules, emotional reinforcers, and hormonal feedback loops that guide the development of social behavior into certain channels as opposed to others. Human nature is not just the array of outcomes attained in existing societies. It is also the potential array that might be achieved through conscious design by future societies. By looking over the realized social systems of hundreds of animal species and deriving the principles by which these systems have evolved, we can be certain that all human choices represent only a tiny subset of those theoretically possible. Human nature is, moreover, a hodgepodge of special genetic adaptations to an environment largely vanished, the world of the Ice-Age hunter-gatherer. Modern life, as rich and rapidly changing as it appears to those caught in it, is nevertheless only a mosaic of cultural hypertrophies of the archaic behavioral adaptations. And at the center of the second dilemma is found a circularity: we are forced to choose among the elements of human nature by reference to value systems which these same elements created in an evolutionary age now long vanished.

Fortunately, this circularity of the human predicament is not so tight that it cannot be broken through an exercise of will. The principal task of human biology is to identify and to measure the constraints that influence the decisions of ethical philosophers and everyone else, and to infer their significance through neurophysiological and phylogenetic reconstructions of the mind. This enterprise is a necessary complement to the continued study of cultural evolution. It will alter the foundation of the social sciences but in no way diminish their richness and importance. In the process it will fashion a biology of ethics, which will make possible the selection of a more deeply understood and enduring code of moral values. . . .

HUMAN GENETICS CAUSES RELIGION

In an analogous manner the mind will always create morality, religion, and mythology and empower them with emotional force. When blind ideologies and religious beliefs are stripped away, others are quickly manufactured as replacements. If the cerebral cortex is rigidly trained in the techniques of critical analysis and packed with tested information, it will reorder all that into some form of morality, religion, and mythology. If the mind is instructed that its pararational activity cannot be combined with the rational, it will divide itself into two compartments so that both activities can continue to flourish side by side.

SOCIETY CANNOT CHANGE HUMAN NATURE

The existence of this tendency to aggression which we can detect in ourselves and rightly presume to be present in others is the factor that disturbs our relations with our neighbours and makes it necessary for culture to institute its high demands. Civilized society is perpetually menaced with disintegration through this primary hostility of men towards one another. Their interests in their common work would not hold them together; the passions of instinct are stronger than reasoned interests. Culture has to call up every possible reinforcement in order to erect barriers against the aggressive instincts of men and hold their manifestations in check by reaction-formations in men's minds. Hence its system of methods by which mankind is to be driven to identifications and aim-inhibited love-relationships; hence the restrictions on sexual life; and hence, too, its ideal command to love one's neighbour as oneself, which is really justified by the fact that nothing is so completely at variance with original human nature as this. With all its striving, this endeavour of culture's has so far not achieved very much. Civilization expects to prevent the worst atrocities of brutal violence by taking upon itself the right to employ violence against criminals, but the law is not able to lay hands on the more discreet and subtle forms in which human aggressions are expressed.

Sigmund Freud, *Civilization and Its Discontents*, 1930.

This mythopoeic drive can be harnessed to learning and the rational search for human progress if we finally concede that scientific materialism is itself a mythology defined in the noble sense. So let me give again the reasons why I consider the scientific ethos superior to religion: its repeated triumphs in explaining and controlling the physical world; its self-correcting nature open to all competent to devise and conduct the tests; its readiness to examine all subjects sacred and profane; and now the possibility of explaining traditional religion by the mechanistic models of evolutionary biology. The last achievement will be crucial. If religion, including the dogmatic secular ideologies, can be systematically analyzed and explained as a product of the brain's evolution, its power as an external source of morality will be gone forever and the solution of the second dilemma will have become a practical necessity.

The core of scientific materialism is the evolutionary epic. Let me repeat its minimum claims: that the laws of the physical sciences are consistent with those of the biological and social sciences and can be linked in chains of causal explanation; that life and mind have a physical basis; that the world as we know it has evolved from earlier worlds obedient to the same laws; and that the visible universe today is everywhere subject to these materialist explanations. The epic can be indefinitely strengthened up and down the line, but its most sweeping assertions cannot be proved with finality.

What I am suggesting, in the end, is that the evolutionary epic is probably the best myth we will ever have. It can be adjusted until it comes as close to truth as the human mind is constructed to judge the truth. And if that is the case, the mythopoeic requirements of the mind must somehow be met by scientific materialism so as to reinvest our superb energies. . . .

NEW EVOLUTIONARY MYTH IS NEEDED

This view will be rejected even more firmly by those whose emotional needs are satisfied by traditional organized religion. God and the church, they will claim, cannot be extinguished ex parte by a rival mythology based on science. They will be right. God remains a viable hypothesis as the prime mover, however undefinable and untestable that conception may be. The rituals of religion, especially the rites of passage and the sanctification of nationhood, are deeply entrenched and incorporate some of the most magnificent elements of existing cultures. They will certainly continue to be practiced long after their etiology has been disclosed. The anguish of death alone will be enough to keep them alive. It would be arrogant to suggest that a belief in a personal, moral God will disappear. . . .

GENETICS GUIDES ALL THINKING

Humanists show a touching faith in the power of knowledge and the idea of evolutionary progress over the minds of men. I am suggesting a modification of scientific humanism through the recognition that the mental processes of religious belief—consecration of personal and group identity, attention to charismatic leaders, mythopoeism, and others—represent programmed predispositions whose self-sufficient components were incorporated into the neural apparatus of the brain by thousands of generations of genetic evolution. As such they are powerful, ineradicable, and at the center of human social existence. They are also structured to a degree not previously appreciated by most philosophers. I suggest further that scientific materialism must accommodate them on two levels: as a scientific puzzle of great complexity and interest, and as a source of energies that can be shifted in new directions when scientific materialism itself is accepted as the more powerful mythology.

That transition will proceed at an accelerating rate. Man's destiny is to know, if only because societies with knowledge culturally dominate societies that lack it. Luddites and anti-intellectuals do not master the differential equations of thermodynamics or the biochemical cures of illness. They stay in thatched huts and die young. Cultures with unifying goals will learn more rapidly than those that lack them, and an autocatalytic growth of learning will follow because scientific materialism is the only mythology that can manufacture great goals from the sustained pursuit of pure knowledge. . . .

GENETICS GUIDES FUTURE POSSIBILITIES

Now there is reason to entertain the view that the culture of each society travels along one or the other of a set of evolutionary trajectories whose full array is constrained by the genetic rules of human nature. While broadly scattered from an anthropocentric point of view, this array still represents only a tiny subset of all the trajectories that would be possible in the absence of the genetic constraints.

As our knowledge of human nature grows, and we start to elect a system of values on a more objective basis, and our minds at last align with our hearts, the set of trajectories will narrow still more. We already know, to take two extreme and opposite examples, that the worlds of William Graham Sumner, the absolute Social Darwinist, and Mikhail Bakunin, the anarchist, are biologically impossible. As the social sciences mature into predictive disciplines, the permissible trajectories will not only diminish in number but our descendants will be able to sight farther along them.

Then mankind will face the third and perhaps final spiritual dilemma. Human genetics is now growing quickly along with all other branches of science. In time, much knowledge concerning the genetic foundation of social behavior will accumulate, and techniques may become available for altering gene complexes by molecular engineering and rapid selection through cloning. At the very least, slow evolutionary change will be feasible through conventional eugenics. The human species can change its own nature. What will it choose? Will it remain the same, teetering on a jerrybuilt foundation of partly obsolete Ice-Age adaptations? Or will it press on toward still higher intelligence and creativity, accompanied by a greater—or lesser—capacity for emotional response?

"What [man] thinks of himself has a pervasive effect on all he does and becomes."

HUMAN NATURE IS FREE AND COMPLEX

George W. Morgan

While many people have attempted to view human nature with the tools of scientific observation, some thinkers have questioned this approach. Although George W. Morgan does not reject science as a useful way of studying humanity, he rejects the idea that science is the only way. Morgan believes that humans are too complex for science to give a complete understanding of human nature. Morgan, in the following viewpoint, challenges the reader to preserve the "wholeness" of human life. This wholeness includes ideas that are difficult to understand, such as freedom and values. Morgan concludes that human nature is filled with tension and complexity.

As you read, consider the following questions:

1. According to Morgan, why is it wrong to "reduce and divide" human nature?
2. Morgan writes that human "freedom is not chaos, chance, or license." According to Morgan, what is freedom?
3. Explain why Morgan believes that "partial or divided" persons cannot relate well to other people.

Excerpted from pp. 320–25 of *The Human Predicament: Dissolution and Wholeness*, by George W. Morgan. Copyright ©1968 by Brown University. Reprinted by permission of the University Press of New England.

B y *whole* I mean both unreduced and undivided. The man who is whole acknowledges and unifies all elements of his human self. He does not try to escape from the complexity and difficulty of human existence by suppressing parts of himself, thus transferring authority from a whole to a partial being; nor does he attempt to resolve this complexity and difficulty by splitting himself into compartments. He is neither a mere part of a social system nor an isolated individualist. The pressures on him and the demands from the world are brought together in a center as rays in a focus, and his approaches to the world issue from this center. He is always himself. . . .

Only if we become capable of taking different approaches to the world and of maintaining constant communion and a living balance among them can we hope to do justice to each moment of life. This is most difficult, for the ways in which we face the world easily become rigid, and to alter these ways is to transform our innermost being. Nothing requires more courage. Nothing is more desperately urgent for modern man. . . .

IMAGES OF HUMANITY

Man cannot be whole if the conceptions he has of himself reduce and divide him, for what he thinks of himself has a pervasive effect on all he does and becomes. To do justice to man, one must not diminish understanding or raise a method above the reality to be apprehended. One must remember that what a person perceives depends on his attitude and that the attitude usually called objectivity is but a special and limited kind of respect; one must respect man fully and see him as the being he is, not reduce him to whatever likenesses he has (no matter how important) to things that are nonhuman. One must overcome the perverse and aggressive desire to degrade man and must not absurdly and stubbornly reverse the ancient error of anthropomorphizing the nonhuman world by dehumanizing man. One must look to various modes of apprehension in order to become aware of man's many aspects and his inexhaustible substance; one must be attentive to and cultivate all the resources of symbols; one must see man in the fullness of his being in the world, especially in the relation of man with man.

To be capable of seeing man thus is itself a manifestation of wholeness. Our striving to transcend the prosaic conception is a part of our striving toward wholeness. What a man believes is an inseparable part of who he is. This multiplies the difficulties of wholeness. But it also gives cause for hope, for whether growth toward wholeness takes place in the way one lives or in the views one holds, growth in the one may enhance the other.

It is not necessary here to give a detailed refutation of the denials of the reality of freedom that are a part of modern conceptions of man. It is sufficient to note that these denials invariably proceed from a prosaic outlook. Man is reduced to what is seen of him by science and quasi science; he is made into an instance of general principles and is supposed to be exhaustively explained, or at least explainable, in explicit symbols. All this, we have seen, is radically mistaken, for what science does not perceive is not therefore nonexistent. Nor do purpose, self-government, and freedom require the negation or suspension of scientific laws. To suppose that they do is to take it for granted that science exhausts the world, to accept a prosaic outlook. To recognize freedom, one must look to other modes of apprehension than science. Freedom belongs to the person and can be known only by an approach that respects the person. We can know freedom in ourself, and we can know it in another through response that acknowledges the other as a person. Freedom resides first of all in the "inside" of human action, and to know it one must therefore be attentive to the inner experience of man.

MAN'S IMAGE OF MAN

Man depends, to a very great degree, on the idea he has of himself and that this idea cannot be degraded without at the same time degrading man.

Gabriel Marcel, *Man Against Mass Society*, n.d.

Freedom is not chaos, chance, or license. Nor is it the individual's separation from the world. On the contrary, it is his capacity to respect the world, to apprehend it, to respond to and be responsible for it, and to judge and decide and engage in action. . . .

Freedom as a capacity, as the power of the self to be in the world, is inseparably linked with wholeness. Any part of the person that is not acknowledged and integrated into a whole, like an outlaw attacks the parts ostensibly in control. In this is to be found the fatal error of those who make a cleavage between the rational and the emotional. Such persons do not acknowledge the emotions and take them into a unified self, but repress them or cast them out and suppose that in their detachment they are free from emotion and therefore rational. Instead, the emotions—prevented from constituting a vital element of the whole—impinge upon thought and curtail its freedom in unrecognized, underground ways. The very doctrine, for example, that in the search for knowledge one must expel emotion, that understanding can only be gained in detachment, is shaped under pressure of unrecognized emotions—not the least of which is fear of emotion and the consequent need to cling to the security of a sterile scheme. Only if the emotions are accepted as fully belonging to the self is it possible to prevent their turning into covert masters. . . .

COMMITMENT AND VALUES

Wholeness makes the difference between commitment and enslavement. Only in freedom can one commit oneself. Any end or activity that is not made answerable to the whole person becomes a prison, for the partial person, who is tied to the end, is incapable of seeing beyond it. The partial person does not choose a given end from among other ends and in view of a total situation but abandons choice and decision, not committing himself but giving himself up. Hence the bonds of commitment are replaced by the bondage of servitude; dedication changes to automatism; devotion becomes compulsion.

Choice and commitment imply valuation, and valuation, like freedom, is linked with wholeness, for when any part of life is segregated from the rest, assessment of that part becomes impossible. Only if one part is balanced with other parts—only if it is seen in concrete context, and if all parts of the world and all parts of the self involved in a particular occasion are acknowledged and reconciled—can there be true valuation. Otherwise values become pseudo values—interests, methods, or goals isolated from all else, set up as values, and blindly affirmed. . . .

THE WHOLE, HEALTHY PERSON

Only a whole self is capable of genuine response, especially to a human being. The partial or divided person is afraid of encounter, afraid to expose his rigid and brittle stability. He cannot summon the courage to listen, to respect the unique, to open himself to the unreducible and unforseeable. He cannot risk himself, because his very existence is tied to division and suppression instead of to a unity in which all elements of the self and its confrontation with the world come together and cohere. Therefore the nonunified person will avoid the other. Distrusting him and being on guard, he will neutralize the potential impact of the other by reducing him to something he can deal with—the embodiment of a function, a commodity, a case, a problem, or a challenge whose conquest will yield reassurance. The divided person will seek to ignore the other entirely, or to ward him off by aggression; he will try to avoid the impact of the other's being by playing a role or by selling himself. A nonunified person cannot acknowledge another because he does not acknowledge himself; he is fearful of being brought up against his own self-betrayal. A whole person has the courage to be open, to risk himself, to be himself, because his being is an embracing unity. The courage to be oneself and the courage to respond to another are inseparable.

HUMAN NATURE IS A MYSTERY

Know then thyself, presume not God to scan;
The proper study of Mankind is Man.
Plac'd on this isthmus of a middle state,
A being darkly wise, and rudely great:
With too much knowledge for the Sceptic side,
With too much weakness for the Stoic's pride,
He hangs between; in doubt to act, or rest,
In doubt to deem himself a God, or Beast;
In doubt his Mind or Body to prefer,
Born but to die, and reas'ning but to err;
Alike in ignorance, his reason such,
Whether he thinks too little, or too much:
Chaos of Thought and Passion, all confus'd;
Still by himself abus'd, or disabus'd;
Created half to rise, and half to fall;
Great lord of all things, yet a prey to all;
Sole judge of Truth, in endless Error hurl'd:
The glory, jest, and riddle of the world!

Alexander Pope, *An Essay on Man*, 1733–34.

For the whole man no activity, goal, method, or interest remains uninformed by true relation to other beings. He assesses and shapes every pursuit with respect and concern for men as men. He allows no transformation of the physical, social, or cultural environment to take place without consideration for persons. Nor does he make business, government, law, medicine, learning, or art into a compartmentalized self-justifying pursuit in which response and responsibility are ignored. But today we avoid response and disavow responsibility, either by appealing to the duties of a job or profession, by disclaiming competence outside our specialty, or by calling on the name of progress. These and other protestations are but ways of hiding in publicly approved shelters, of escaping from the complexity of human life into simple and comforting solutions and keeping the self untouched by others; they are ways of avoiding the weight and risk of freedom and judgment, and hence the responsibility for ourself and others—in short, of evading the burden of being whole. To respond to others and be responsible for them is the very essence of being a man.

The wholeness of the person is not simple. Man's interests, values, needs, faculties, and approaches to the world are varied and cannot be harmonized easily. The unified self must encompass tensions, frictions, and contrarieties.

| "Man is free and . . . there is no
human nature for me to depend on."

THERE IS NO HUMAN NATURE

Jean-Paul Sartre

Jean-Paul Sartre (1905–1980) was a French philosopher and literary figure. During World War II and in the following years, he
served as an intellectual leader of a philosophy called existentialism. In the following excerpt from his book *Existentialism*, he suggests that the concept of human nature belongs to earlier conceptions of humanity. When people assumed that God existed
and that this God revealed his thoughts to humanity, it was reasonable to believe that God had some sort of general concept of
humanity of which each person was a unique example. But
Sartre is confident that God does not exist, and so concludes that
human nature also does not exist. Even if God exists, Sartre assumes that we have no revelation from God to guide our values,
our actions, or our self-understanding. Thus, Sartre believes all
humans share the heavy burden of responsibility for how they
create themselves. As individuals and as a race, humans must accept the responsibility of defining their essential nature.

As you read, consider the following questions:

1. What does Sartre mean by the phrase, "existence precedes
   essence"?
2. What are the two kinds of subjectivism?
3. Why does Sartre say that we cannot predict human behavior
   and that humans have no excuses?

A theistic existentialism, which I represent, is more coherent. It states that if God does not exist, there is at least one being in whom existence precedes essence, a being who exists before he can be defined by any concept, and that this being is man, or, as [German philosopher Martin] Heidegger says, human reality. What is meant here by saying that existence precedes essence? It means that, first of all, man exists, turns up, appears on the scene, and, only afterwards, defines himself. If man, as the existentialist conceives him, is indefinable, it is because at first he is nothing. Only afterward will he be something, and he himself will have made what he will be. Thus, there is no human nature, since there is no God to conceive it. Not only is man what he conceives himself to be, but he is also only what he wills himself to be after this thrust toward existence.

MAN MAKES HIMSELF

Man is nothing else but what he makes of himself. Such is the first principle of existentialism. It is also what is called subjectivity, the name we are labeled with when charges are brought against us. But what do we mean by this, if not that man has a greater dignity than a stone or table? For we mean that man first exists, that is, that man first of all is the being who hurls himself toward a future and who is conscious of imagining himself as being in the future. Man is at the start a plan which is aware of itself, rather than a patch of moss, a piece of garbage, or a cauliflower; nothing exists prior to this plan; there is nothing in heaven; man will be what he will have planned to be. Not what he will want to be. Because by the word "will" we generally mean a conscious decision, which is subsequent to what we have already made of ourselves. I may want to belong to a political party, write a book, get married; but all that is only a manifestation of an earlier, more spontaneous choice that is called "will." But if existence really does precede essence, man is responsible for what he is. Thus, existentialism's first move is to make every man aware of what he is and to make the full responsibility of his existence rest on him. And when we say that a man is responsible for himself, we do not only mean that he is responsible for his own individuality, but that he is responsible for all men.

SUBJECTIVISM

The word subjectivism has two meanings, and our opponents play on the two. Subjectivism means, on the one hand, that an individual chooses and makes himself; and, on the other, that it is impossible for man to transcend human subjectivity. The second of these is the essential meaning of existentialism. When we say that man chooses his own self, we mean that every one of us does likewise; but we also mean by that that in making this choice he also chooses all men. In fact, in creating the man that we want to be, there is not a single one of our acts which does not at the same time create an image of man as we think he ought to be. To choose to be this or that is to affirm at the same time the value of what we choose, because we can never choose evil. We always choose the good, and nothing can be good for us without being good for all.

"Jumping Over Our Own Shadows"

The problem of human nature, the Augustinian *quaestio mihi factus sum* ("a question have I become for myself"), seems unanswerable in both its individual psychological sense and its general philosophical sense. It is highly unlikely that we, who can know, determine, and define the natural essences of all things surrounding us, which we are not, should ever be able to do the same for ourselves—this would be like jumping over our own shadows. Moreover, nothing entitles us to assume that man has a nature or essence in the same sense as other things. In other words, if we have a nature or essence, then surely only a god could know and define it.

Hannah Arendt, *The Human Condition*, 1958.

If, on the other hand, existence precedes essence, and if we grant that we exist and fashion our image at one and the same time, the image is valid for everybody and for our whole age. Thus, our responsibility is much greater than we might have supposed, because it involves all mankind. . . .

We Have No Excuses

The existentialist, on the contrary, thinks it very distressing that God does not exist, because all possibility of finding values in a heaven of ideas disappears along with Him; there can no longer be an *a priori* Good, since there is no infinite and perfect consciousness to think it. Nowhere is it written that the Good exists, that we must be honest, that we must not lie; because the fact is we are on a plane where there are only men. [Russian novelist Fyodor] Dostoievsky said, "If God didn't exist, everything would be possible." That is the very starting point of existentialism. Indeed, everything is permissible if God does not exist, and as a result man is forlorn, because neither within him nor without does he find anything to cling to. He can't start making excuses for himself.

If existence really does precede essence, there is no explaining things away by reference to a fixed and given human nature. In other words, there is no determinism, man is free, man is freedom. On the other hand, if God does not exist, we find no values or commands to turn to which legitimize our conduct. So, in the bright realm of values, we have no excuse behind us, nor justification before us. We are alone, with no excuses.

That is the idea I shall try to convey when I say that man is condemned to be free. Condemned, because he did not create himself, yet, in other respects is free; because, once thrown into the world, he is responsible for everything he does. . . .

WE CANNOT PREDICT HUMAN BEHAVIOR

But, given that man is free and that there is no human nature for me to depend on, I can not count on men whom I do not know by relying on human goodness or man's concern for the good of society. I don't know what will become of the Russian revolution; I may make an example of it to the extent that at the present time it is apparent that the proletariat plays a part in Russia that it plays in no other nation. But I can't swear that this will inevitably lead to a triumph of the proletariat. I've got to limit myself to what I see.

CONDEMNED TO CONSTANTLY CHANGING

Just as there is no eternal ideal pattern of culture, there is no such pattern of man. By assuming a different form in every culture, man is not deviating from a form he should have. As variability is the law of culture, so it is the law of man. In fact, it is a law of culture only because it is one of man. Man does not have an intrinsic being that remains immutably the same, while history unrolls only in the outer regions. Even for spontaneous actions apparently independent of history, such as loving and praying, we have no guidelines valid once and for all as to how we should perform them: down to our deepest interior we are committed to a fate of historical mutability.

Michael Landmann, *Philosophical Anthropology*, 1974.

Given that men are free and that tomorrow they will freely decide what man will be, I can not be sure that, after my death, fellow-fighters will carry on my work to bring it to its maximum perfection. Tomorrow, after my death, some men may decide to set up Fascism, and the others may be cowardly and muddled enough to let them do it. Fascism will then be the human reality, so much the worse for us.

Actually, things will be as man will have decided they are to be. Does that mean that I should abandon myself to quietism? No. First, I should involve myself; then, act on the old saw, "Nothing ventured, nothing gained.". . . Quietism is the attitude of people who say, "Let others do what I can't do." The doctrine I am presenting is the very opposite of quietism, since it declares, "There is no reality except in action." Moreover, it goes further, since it adds, "Man is nothing else than his plan; he exists only to the extent that he fulfills himself; he is therefore nothing else than the ensemble of his acts, nothing else than his life.". . .

THE HUMAN CONDITION

Besides, if it is impossible to find in every man some universal essence which would be human nature, yet there does exist a universal human condition. It's not by chance that today's thinkers speak more readily of man's condition than of his nature. By condition they mean, more or less definitely, the *a priori* limits which outline man's fundamental situation in the universe. Historical situations vary; a man may be born a slave in a pagan society or a feudal lord or a proletarian. What does not vary is the necessity for him to exist in the world, to be at work there, to be there in the midst of other people, and to be mortal there.

| "A denial of human nature is rooted
in a profound mistake."

THERE IS A HUMAN NATURE

Mortimer J. Adler

Mortimer J. Adler is a unique philosopher. He has written and edited a large number of books bringing together knowledge from many fields of human thought. For example, his massive *The Idea of Freedom* is an attempt to show how theologians, philosophers, psychologists, and political theorists have used this term throughout history. His emphasis on the uniqueness of human nature can be found in such books as: *What Man Has Made of Man* and *The Difference of Man and the Difference It Makes*. Adler is also unique in his efforts to make philosophy understandable to average readers. This excerpt is taken from his popular work, *Ten Philosophical Mistakes*. Adler understands why some people are tempted to reject the idea of human nature, yet he argues that there is in fact a common nature found in all humans.

As you read, consider the following questions:

1. According to Adler, why do many people doubt the existence of human nature?
2. What does the author mean by "human potentialities"?
3. How does Adler explain the difference between animals and humans?

In the twentieth century, the essential sameness of all human beings, by virtue of their participating in the same specific nature, has been widely challenged. The challenge has come from cultural anthropologists, from sociologists, from other behavioral scientists, and even from historians.

That challenge, tantamount to a denial of human nature, is rooted in a profound mistake, but one that is not, in origin at least, a philosophical mistake. However, it should be added that philosophers have not been at pains to correct the error and that it has become for some philosophers—the existentialists—the root error in their thought. [French philosopher Maurice] Merleau-Ponty, for example, has declared that "it is the nature of man not to have a nature.". . .

At this point readers may call for a pause and an explanation. What can possibly be meant by the denial of human nature? We are all human beings, are we not? It must be extremely rare, if it ever happened at all, that anyone would have some doubt about whether a specimen being examined was human or not.

This being so, do not the criteria we employ to determine whether we are dealing with a human being imply some understanding on our part of the common traits belonging to all members of the human species? These common traits constitute the nature that is the same in all members of the species. That is what we mean by human nature, is it not? . . .

ALL HUMANS ARE DIFFERENT

Of course human beings, like other animals, must eat, drink, and sleep. They all have certain biological traits in common. There can be no doubt that they have the nature of animals. But when you come to their human traits, how different one human population will be from another.

They will differ in the languages they speak, and you will have some difficulty in making an accurate count of the vast number of different languages you will have found.

They will differ in their dress, in their adornments, in their cuisines, in their customs and manners, in the organization of their families, in the institutions of their societies, in their beliefs, in their standards of conduct, in the turn of their minds, in almost everything that enters into the ways of life they lead. These differences will be so multitudinous and variegated that you might, unless cautioned against doing so, tend to be persuaded that they were not all members of the same species.

In any case, you cannot avoid being persuaded that, in the human case, membership in the same species does not carry with it the dominant similitude that you would find in the case of other animal species. On the contrary, the differences between one human race and another, between one racial variety and another, between one ethnic group and another, between one nation and another, would seem to be dominant.

It is this that might lead you to the conclusion that there is no human nature in the sense in which a certain constant nature can be attributed to other species of animals. . . .

Looked at one way, the denial of human nature is correct. The members of the human species do not have a specific or common nature in the same sense that the members of other animal species do. This, by the way, is one of the most remarkable differences between man and other animals, one that tends to corroborate the conclusion that man differs from other animals in kind, not in degree.

But to concede that the members of the human species do not have a specific or common nature in the same sense that the members of other animal species do is not to admit that they have no specific nature whatsoever. An alternative remains open; namely, that the members of the human species all have the same nature in a quite different sense.

In what sense then is there a human nature, a specific nature that is common to all members of the species? The answer can be given in a single word: potentialities. Human nature is constituted by all the potentialities that are the species-specific properties common to all members of the human species.

It is the essence of a potentiality to be capable of a wide variety of different actualizations. Thus, for example, the human potentiality for syntactical speech is actualized in thousands of different human languages. Having that potentiality, a human infant placed at the moment of birth in one or another human subgroup, each with its own language, would learn to speak that language. The differences among all human languages are superficial as compared with the potentiality for learning and speaking any human language that is present in all human infants at birth.

Unity in Diversity

What has just been said about one human potentiality applies to all the others that are the common, specific traits of the human being. Each underlies all the differences that arise among human subgroups as a result of the many different ways in which the same potentiality can be actualized. To recognize this is tantamount to acknowledging the superficiality of the differences that separate one human subgroup from another, as compared with the samenesses that unite all human beings as members of the same species and as having the same specific nature.

HUMAN NATURE HAS INFINITE POSSIBILITIES

Human nature may contract or expand. Or, rather, human nature is rooted in infinity and has access to boundless energy. But man's consciousness may be narrowed down and repressed. . . . Insofar as human nature is narrowed down by consciousness it becomes shallow and unreceptive. It feels cut off from the sources of creative energy. What makes man interesting and significant is that his mind has, so to speak, an opening into infinity. But average normal consciousness tries to close this opening, and then man finds it difficult to manifest all his gifts and resources of creative energy.

Nicolas Berdyaev, *The Destiny of Man*, 1937.

In other species of animals, the samenesses that unite the members and constitute their common nature are not potentialities but rather quite determinate characteristics, behavioral as well as anatomical and physiological. This accounts for the impression derived from studying these other species—the impression of a dominant similitude among its members.

Turning to the human species, the opposite impression of dominant differences among subgroups can also be accounted for. The explanation of it lies in the fact that, as far as behavioral characteristics are concerned, the common nature all the subgroups share consists entirely of species-specific potentialities. These are actualized by these subgroups in all the different ways that we find when we make a global study of mankind.

MISTAKES IN SOCIAL SCIENCES

A newcomer to the behavioral sciences, sociobiology, has tried to show that to a significant extent animal and human behavior is genetically determined. So far as the human species is concerned, what little truth there is in sociobiology applies only to the genetic determination of human potentialities, not to their behavioral development.

The mistake that the cultural anthropologists, the sociologists, and other behavioral scientists make when they deny the existence of human nature has its root in their failure to understand that the specific nature in the case of the human species is radically different from the specific nature in the case of other animal species. . . .

Human Nature Is Hidden

Man is to a great extent a self-made creature. Given a range of potentialities at birth, he makes himself what he becomes by how he freely chooses to develop those potentialities by the habits he forms.

It is thus that differentiated subgroups of human beings came into existence. Once in existence, they subsequently affected the way in which those born into these subgroups came to develop the acquired characteristics that differentiate one subgroup from another. These acquired characteristics, especially the behavioral ones, are the results of acculturation; or, even more generally, results of the way in which those born into this or that subgroup are nurtured differently.

No other animal is a self-made creature in the sense indicated above. On the contrary, other animals have determinate natures, natures genetically determined in such a way that they do not admit of a wide variety of different developments as they mature.

Human nature is also genetically determined; but, because the genetic determination consists, behaviorally, in an innate endowment of potentialities that are determinable in different ways, human beings differ remarkably from one another as they mature. . . .

All the cultural and nurtural differences that separate one human subgroup from another are superficial as compared with the underlying common human nature that unites the members of mankind.

Although our samenesses are more important than our differences, we have an inveterate tendency to stress the differences that divide us rather than the samenesses that unite us.

WHAT CONSTITUTES HUMAN NATURE?

CHAPTER PREFACE

An interesting feature of most discussions about human nature is an underlying dissatisfaction with the present state of humanity. Writers continue to ponder why humans fight wars, why people are cruel to each other, and why tensions constantly alienate humans from each other.

British philosopher Thomas Hobbes assumes that humans are selfish and warlike by nature. The only way to curb the destructive nature of humanity, then, is to have a strong government. Such a government wins the respect and obedience of the people by harshly punishing the antisocial behavior that is natural to humans. As a result, humans learn to suppress their natural tendencies.

In stark contrast to Hobbes, philosopher Jean-Jacques Rousseau states that humans are naturally innocent. This is not to say that Rousseau is satisfied with humanity; on the contrary, Rousseau regrets the present state of humanity, which he argues is unnatural. As society has evolved, so has humanity's difficulties. Originally, humans lived as lone individuals in a state of innocence. As time passed, however, society became more and more complex and humans became more and more corrupted by greed, material things, and social expectations. Rousseau regrets that humanity's original purity cannot be regained. Humanity cannot return to its earlier stage of innocent individualism or its earlier relationship with nature.

Sigmund Freud agrees with Rousseau that humans do not naturally enjoy social living. Freud views society as something imposed on individuals against their true nature. However, Freud comes to a very different conclusion about the natural state of humanity. In contrast to Rousseau, Freud believes that humans are instinctively aggressive. Freud explains that humans live together in social groups to survive and to meet their needs, not by natural inclination. The natural tendency of people is to rebel against social pressures and to act aggressively toward all others who are viewed as threats. Freud does not allude to the evolution of humanity or to an early state of harmony with nature, as does Rousseau; however, both see humanity torn between individualistic urges and social dependence.

In contrast to Rousseau and Freud, Riane Eisler is hopeful when she looks at human nature. Eisler believes that humanity began with cooperative societies but later became competitive, aggressive, and destructive. Similar to Rousseau, Eisler argues that the original nature of humanity was quite innocent and peaceful. Eisler, however, is hopeful that the negative features of social evolution can be reversed and humanity can learn to live in harmony once again. Eisler does not see a fixed conflict between humanity's instincts and social living.

The book of Genesis also proposes an original human innocence. God created the first man and woman and they were part of a world that was "very good." That innocence was lost when Adam and Eve disobeyed God. The Genesis account shows that the first sin destroyed more than the innocence of humanity. The relationship between humanity and God was harmed, the relationship between man and woman was altered, and the relationship between humanity and nature was no longer harmonious. The story of Cain and Abel, which follows the description of creation, suggests a further decline of humanity. The first child of Adam and Eve is a murderer. Cain was given the choice between doing what was right and the temptation "crouching at your door." He fails and kills his brother. The early chapters of Genesis suggest that human nature has been corrupted in a number of ways.

The theories of naturalist Charles Darwin greatly contrast the story of Genesis and the origin of humanity. Darwin saw a unity between human and animal behavior that was lacking in Genesis. Rather than falling from a height of purity and goodness, Darwin presents humanity as the culmination of a long evolutionary process. However, Darwin is not satisfied with some of humanity's behaviors. Darwin explains that any improvement of humanity must begin with an understanding of humanity's evolution and its close relationship with the animals.

Although the viewpoints in this chapter offer extremely different perspectives on human nature, they agree on at least one point: Humans in their present state are flawed.

I "Every man is enemy to every man."

HUMAN NATURE IS ANTISOCIAL

Thomas Hobbes

Thomas Hobbes (1588–1679) was an English philosopher of
political theory. He began his thinking by asking: Why do humans need government? His answer was that humans are naturally at war with each other. Only government forces people
into a state of peace. Because humans are constantly fearful of
what others might do to them, they submit to a government. He
concludes that only artificial political systems can force people
to cooperate with each other.

As you read, consider the following questions:
1. Why does Hobbes believe that mental and physical equality
   leads to conflicts between people?
2. According to Hobbes, what are the three causes of quarrels
   between people?
3. Why does the state of war keep people from making progress
   in industry and commerce?

Reprinted from Thomas Hobbes, *Leviathan*, Part I, chapter 13 (London: 1651).

N ature has made men so equal in the faculties of the body and mind as that, though there be found one man sometimes manifestly stronger in body or of quicker mind than another, yet, when all is reckoned together, the difference between man and man is not so considerable as that one man can thereupon claim to himself any benefit to which another may not pretend as well as he. For as to the strength of body, the weakest has strength enough to kill the strongest, either by secret machination or by confederacy with others that are in the same danger with himself. . . .

EQUALITY LEADS TO TENSIONS

For prudence is but experience, which equal time equally bestows on all men in those things they equally apply themselves unto. That which may perhaps make such equality incredible is but a vain conceit of one's own wisdom, which almost all men think they have in a greater degree than the vulgar—that is, than all men but themselves and a few others whom, by fame or for concurring with themselves, they approve. For such is the nature of men that howsoever they may acknowledge many others to be more witty or more eloquent or more learned, yet they will hardly believe there be many so wise as themselves; for they see their own wit at hand and other men's at a distance. But this proves rather that men are in that point equal than unequal. For there is not ordinarily a greater sign of the equal distribution of anything than that every man is contented with his share.

From this equality of ability arises equality of hope in the attaining of our ends. And therefore if any two men desire the same thing, which nevertheless they cannot both enjoy, they become enemies; and in the way to their end, which is principally their own conservation, and sometimes their delectation only, endeavor to destroy or subdue one another. And from hence it comes to pass that where an invader has no more to fear than another man's single power, if one plant, sow, build, or possess a convenient seat, others may probably be expected to come prepared with forces united to dispossess and deprive him, not only of the fruit of his labor, but also of his life or liberty. And the invader again is in the like danger of another. . . .

CONFLICT IS NATURAL

So that in the nature of man we find three principal causes of quarrel: first, competition; secondly, diffidence; thirdly, glory.

The first makes men invade for gain, the second for safety, and the third for reputation. The first use violence to make themselves masters of other men's persons, wives, children, and cattle; the second, to defend them; the third, for trifles, as a word, a smile, a different opinion, and any other sign of under-value, either direct in their persons or by reflection in their kindred, their friends, their nation, their profession, or their name.

Hereby it is manifest that, during the time men live without a common power to keep them all in awe, they are in that condition which is called war, and such a war as is of every man against every man. For WAR consists not in battle only, or the act of fighting, but in a tract of time wherein the will to contend by battle is sufficiently known; and therefore the notion of *time* is to be considered in the nature of war as it is in the nature of weather. For as the nature of foul weather lies not in a shower or two of rain but in an inclination thereto of many days together, so the nature of war consists not in actual fighting but in the known disposition thereto during all the time there is no assurance to the contrary. All other time is PEACE.

CONFLICT MAKES PROGRESS IMPOSSIBLE

Whatsoever, therefore, is consequent to a time of war where every man is enemy to every man, the same is consequent to the time wherein men live without other security than what their own strength and their own invention shall furnish them withal. In such condition there is no place for industry, because the fruit thereof is uncertain: and consequently no culture of the earth; no navigation nor use of the commodities that may be imported by sea; no commodious building; no instruments of moving and removing such things as require much force; no knowledge of the face of the earth; no account of time; no arts; no letters; no society; and, which is worst of all, continual fear and danger of violent death; and the life of man solitary, poor, nasty, brutish, and short.

HUMANS DO NOT TRUST EACH OTHER

It may seem strange to some man that has not well weighed these things that nature should thus dissociate and render men apt to invade and destroy one another; and he may therefore, not trusting to this inference made from the passions, desire perhaps to have the same confirmed by experience. Let him therefore consider with himself—when taking a journey he arms himself and seeks to go well accompanied, when going to sleep he locks his doors, when even in his house he locks his chests, and this when he knows there be laws and public officers, armed, to revenge all injuries shall be done him—what opinion he has of his fellow subjects when he rides armed, of his fellow citizens when he locks his doors, and of his children and servants when he locks his chests. Does he not there as much accuse mankind by his actions as I do by my words? But neither of us accuse man's nature in it. The desires and other passions of man are in themselves no sin. No more are the actions that proceed from those passions till they know a law that forbids them, which, till laws be made, they cannot know, nor can any law be made till they have agreed upon the person that shall make it.

WILL TO POWER GUIDES ALL BEHAVIOR

Unitary conception of psychology.—We are accustomed to consider the development of an immense abundance of forms compatible with an origin in unity.

[My theory would be:—] that the will to power is the primitive form of affect, that all other affects are only developments of it;

that it is notably enlightening to posit *power* in place of individual "happiness" (after which every living thing is supposed to be striving): "there is a striving for power, for an increase of power";—pleasure is only a symptom of the feeling of power attained, a consciousness of a difference (—there is no striving for pleasure: but pleasure supervenes when that which is being striven for is attained: pleasure is an accompaniment, pleasure is not the motive—);

that all driving force is will to power, that there is no other physical, dynamic or psychic force except this.

Friedrich Nietzsche, *The Will to Power*, 1888.

It may peradventure be thought there was never such a time nor condition of war as this, and I believe it was never generally so over all the world; but there are many places where they live so now. For the savage people in many places of America, except the government of small families, the concord whereof depends on natural lust, have no government at all and live at this day in that brutish manner as I said before. Howsoever, it may be perceived what manner of life there would be where there were no common power to fear by the manner of life which men that have formerly lived under a peaceful government use to degenerate into in a civil war.

But though there had never been any time wherein particular men were in a condition of war one against another, yet in all times kings and persons of sovereign authority, because of their independency, are in continual jealousies and in the state and posture of gladiators, having their weapons pointing and their eyes fixed on one another—that is, their forts, garrisons, and guns upon the frontiers of their kingdoms, and continual spies upon their neighbors—which is a posture of war. But because they uphold thereby the industry of their subjects, there does not follow from it that misery which accompanies the liberty of particular men.

LAWS FORCE HUMANS TO BE GOOD

To this war of every man against every man, this also is consequent: that nothing can be unjust. The notions of right and wrong, justice and injustice, have there no place. Where there is no common power, there is no law; where no law, no injustice. Force and fraud are in war the two cardinal virtues. Justice and injustice are none of the faculties neither of the body nor mind. If they were, they might be in a man that were alone in the world, as well as his senses and passions. They are qualities that relate to men in society, not in solitude. It is consequent also to the same condition that there be no propriety, no dominion, no mine and thine distinct; but only that to be every man's that he can get, and for so long as he can keep it. And thus much for the ill condition which man by mere nature is actually placed in, though with a possibility to come out of it consisting partly in the passions, partly in his reason.

The passions that incline men to peace are fear of death, desire of such things as are necessary to commodious living, and a hope by their industry to obtain them. And reason suggests convenient articles of peace, upon which men may be drawn to agreement. These articles are they which otherwise are called the Laws of Nature.

> "Savage man and civilized man differ
> so much in the depths of their
> hearts and in their inclinations that
> what constitutes the supreme
> happiness of one would reduce the
> other to despair."

HUMAN NATURE IS CORRUPTED BY SOCIETY

Jean-Jacques Rousseau

The ideas of Jean-Jacques Rousseau (1712–1778) marked a shift toward an intellectual and artistic movement called Romanticism. Rousseau, who lived in Switzerland and France, rejected Hobbes' negative views of humanity. Rousseau viewed early humanity as innocent, strong, and free. Hobbes thought that civilization was good, because it controlled the antisocial nature within humanity. In contrast, Rousseau believed that civilization, though inevitable, was destructive. As society has advanced, humans have become more and more enslaved and corrupted by the trappings of civilization.

As you read, consider the following questions:

1. According to Rousseau, in what ways are humans and animals similar? In what ways are they different?
2. According to the author, what problems have humans brought on themselves?
3. Describe how Rousseau views the natural state of humanity.

From *Rousseau's Political Writings: A Norton Critical Edition*, by Alan Ritter and Julia Conaway Bondanella, editors, translated by Julia Conaway Bondanella. Translation copyright ©1988 by W. W. Norton & Company, Inc. Reprinted by permission of W. W. Norton & Company, Inc.

O Man, from whatever country you come, whatever your opinions may be, listen: here is your history as I thought I read it, not in the books of your fellow men, which are deceptive, but in nature, which never lies. All that comes from nature will be true; nothing will be false except what I have involuntarily put there on my own. The times of which I am going to speak are very remote. How much you have changed from what you once were! It is, so to speak, the life of your species that I am going to describe to you in accordance with the qualities which you received and which your education and habits could corrupt but not destroy. There is, I feel, an age at which the individual man would like to remain; you shall seek the age at which you would have desired your species to remain. Discontent with your present state, for reasons which promise still greater unhappiness for your unfortunate posterity, perhaps you would like to have the power to go back, and this sentiment will celebrate your early ancestors, criticize your contemporaries, and frighten those who will have the misfortune to follow you. . . .

DIFFERENCES BETWEEN HUMANS AND ANIMALS

By considering him, in a word, as he must have come from the hands of nature, I see an animal less strong than some, less agile than others, but, on the whole, the most advantageously constituted of all; I see him eating his fill under an oak tree, quenching his thirst at the first stream, making his bed at the foot of the same tree which furnished his meal, with all his needs satisfied.

Left to its natural fertility and covered with immense forests that the axe has never mutilated, the earth offers at every step stores of food and shelter to animals of every species. The men dispersed among them observe and imitate their industry, and thus attain the instincts of the beasts, with the advantage that, unlike any other species which has only its own instinct, man, who has none which belongs to him alone, appropriates them all, lives equally well on most of the different foods that the other animals share among themselves, and, consequently, finds his subsistence more easily than any of them.

Accustomed from infancy to bad weather and the harshness of the seasons, inured to fatigue, and forced, naked and unarmed, to defend their lives and their prey from other wild beasts, or to escape from them by running, men acquire a robust and almost unalterable constitution; the children, bringing into the world with them the excellent constitution of their parents fortifying it by the same exercises that produced it, thus acquire all the vigor of which the human species is capable. Nature treats them precisely as the law of Sparta treated the children of citizens; it makes strong and robust those with good constitutions. . . .

NATURAL STATE IS HEALTH

The extreme inequality in the manner of living, the excessive idleness of some, the excessive labor of others, the ease of exciting and satisfying our appetites and our sensual desires, the overly refined foods of the rich, which nourish them with constipating sauces and prostrate them with indigestion, the bad food of the poor, which they more often lack than not, so that they greedily overburden their stomachs whenever they can, late nights, excesses of every kind, immoderate outbursts of all the passions, hardships, spiritual exhaustion, innumerable pains and afflictions which are felt in every class, and which keep our souls in perpetual torment—this is the deadly proof that most of our ailments are of our own making, and that we could have avoided nearly all of them by preserving the simple, uniform, and solitary manner of living which was prescribed for us by nature. . . .

Let us, therefore, guard against confusing savage man with the men we have before our eyes. Nature treats all the animals left to its care with a partiality that seems to show how jealous it is of this right. The horse, the cat, the bull, even the ass are generally taller, and all have a more robust constitution, more vigor, strength, and courage in the forests than in our homes; they lose half these advantages as they become domesticated, and it could be said that all our efforts to treat these animals well and to feed them serve only to debase them. It is thus with man himself. As he becomes sociable and a slave, he becomes weak, timid, and servile; his soft and effeminate manner of living completely exhausts both his strength and his courage. Let us add that between the savage and domestic conditions the differences from man to man must be even greater than that from beast to beast, for although the animals and man have been treated alike by nature, man gives himself more conveniences than the animals he tames, and these conveniences become so many special causes which make his degeneration more perceptible. . . .

HUMANS HAVE UNIQUE FREEDOM

In every animal, I see only an ingenious machine to which nature has given the senses to maintain its own strength and to protect itself, up to a certain point, from all that tends to disturb it or to destroy it. I perceive precisely the same things in the human machine, with the difference that, whereas nature alone does everything in the operations of the beast, man cooperates in his own as a free agent. The one chooses or rejects through instinct, and the other through a free act; this means that the beast cannot deviate from the rule prescribed for it, even when it would be advantageous to do so, and that man often deviates from his own rule to his detriment. Thus, a pigeon would die of hunger near a dish filled with the choicest meats, and a cat on a heap of fruit or grain, although either could very well live on the food that it disdains, if it had only thought of trying it; thus, dissolute men give themselves over to excesses, which bring on fever and death, because the mind depraves the senses and the will still speaks when nature is silent.

Every animal has ideas because it has senses; it even combines its ideas up to a certain point, and, in this regard, man differs from beasts only in degree. Some philosophers have even claimed that there is a greater difference between one man and another than between a certain man and a certain beast; it is, therefore, not so much the understanding which constitutes the specific difference between man and the animals as his capacity as a free agent. Nature commands every animal and the beast obeys. Man feels the same impulsion, but he knows that he is free to acquiesce or to resist; and it is particularly in the consciousness of this liberty that the spirituality of his soul is displayed, for physics in some way explains the mechanism of the senses and the formation of ideas, but, in the power of willing, or rather of choosing, and in the consciousness of this power, there are only purely mental acts, which cannot be explained by the laws of mechanics. . . .

NATURAL COMPASSION AND INNOCENCE

It is, therefore, very certain that compassion is a natural sentiment, which, by moderating the activity of self-esteem in each individual, contributes to the mutual preservation of the whole species. It carries us without thinking to the aid of those whom we see suffering; in the state of nature it takes the place of laws, moral habits, and virtue, with the advantage that no one is tempted to disobey its gentle voice; it will deter any robust savage from depriving a weak child or an infirm old man of the subsistence he has with great difficulty acquired, if he himself hopes to be able to find his own elsewhere. Instead of that sublime maxim of rational justice, *Do unto others as you would have them do unto you*, it inspires in all men that other maxim of natural goodness, much less perfect but perhaps more useful than the preceding one: *Do what is good for you with the least possible harm to others*. It is, in a word, in this natural sentiment rather than in any subtle arguments that we must seek cause of the repugnance every man would feel in doing evil, even independently of the maxims of education. . . .

THE MEASURE OF MAN

Man's ingenuity has outrun his intelligence. He was good enough to survive in a simple, sparsely populated world, where he was neither powerful enough nor in sufficiently close contact with his neighbors to do them or himself fatal harm. He is not good enough to manage the more complicated and closely integrated world which he is, for the first time, powerful enough to destroy. . . .

We have educated ourselves out of certain ideas necessary to our survival, and that modern thought, like modern technology, has been busy chiefly with the preparation of instruments for an efficient as well as spectacular spiritual suicide calculated to occur at about the same time that the physical world is destroyed.

Joseph Woodkrutch, *The Measure of Man*, 1953.

Let us conclude that, wandering in the forests, without industry, without speech, without shelter, without war, and without ties, with no need of his fellow men, nor any desire to harm them, perhaps without ever even recognizing anyone individually, savage man, self-sufficient and subject to few passions, had only the sentiments and knowledge appropriate to that state; that he felt only his true needs and looked only at what he believed he had an interest in seeing; and that his intelligence made no more progress than his vanity. If by chance he made some discovery, he was all the less able to communicate it, because he did not even recognize his own children. Art perished with the inventor, there was neither education nor progress; the generations multiplied uselessly; and since each generation always started out from the same point, centuries passed by in all the crudeness of the early epochs; the species was already old, and man remained ever a child. . . .

CIVILIZATION CORRUPTS HUMANITY

The first man who, having fenced off a plot of land, thought of saying "This is mine" and found people simple enough to believe him was the real founder of civil society. How many crimes, wars, murders, how many miseries and horrors might the human race have been spared by the one who, upon pulling up the stakes or filling in the ditch, had shouted to his fellow men, "Beware of listening to this imposter; you are lost, if you forget that the fruits of the earth belong to all and that the earth belongs to no one." But by that time, things had very probably already come to the point where they could no longer go on as they were, for this idea of property, depending upon many prior ideas which could only have arisen successively, did not suddenly take shape in the human mind. It was necessary to make much progress, to acquire considerable ingenuity and knowledge, and to transmit and increase them from age to age. . . .

As ideas and feelings succeed one another, and as the mind and heart are trained, the human species continues to be domesticated, contacts increase, and bonds are tightened. People became used to assembling in front of their huts or around a large tree. Song and dance, true children of love and leisure, became the amusement, or rather the occupation of idle men and women gathered together. Each one began to consider the others and to want to be considered in return, and public esteem came to have a value. Anyone who sang or danced the best, who was the most handsome, the strongest, the most skillful, or the most eloquent became the most highly regarded, and this was the first step toward inequality and, at the same time, toward vice. From these first preferences vanity and contempt were born on the one hand, and shame and envy on the other; and the fermentation caused by these new leavens finally produced compounds fatal to happiness and innocence. . . .

In short, he will explain how the soul and human passions, deteriorating imperceptibly, change in nature, so to speak; why the objects of our needs and pleasures change in the long run; why the original man vanished by degrees; and why society offers nothing more to the sage's eyes than an assemblage of unnatural men and artificial passions which are the handiwork of all these new relations and have no real foundation in nature. What reflection teaches us about that, observation confirms perfectly: savage man and civilized man differ so much in the depths of their hearts and in their inclinations that what constitutes the supreme happiness of one would reduce the other to despair. The former breathes only peace and liberty; he wants only to live and to remain at leisure, and even the Stoic's ataraxia falls far short of his profound indifference to every other object. The always active citizen, on the contrary, sweats, struggles, torments himself constantly to seek out still more laborious occupations. He toils until death; he even hurries toward it to enable himself to live, or he renounces life to acquire immortality.

| "Civilization has to use its utmost efforts in order to set limits to man's aggressive instincts."

HUMAN NATURE IS AGGRESSIVE

Sigmund Freud

In the first half of the twentieth century, Sigmund Freud (1856–1939) established psychoanalysis as a source from which people could understand themselves and others. For many people psychoanalysts became like secular priests, helping people deal with the personal and social tensions they felt in their lives. Most of Freud's work was aimed at understanding individual people. However, in *Civilization and Its Discontents* Freud tried to help his readers understand the larger social forces which affect human behavior. Freud views human nature as torn by irresolvable tensions. In the following selection, Freud contends that even though people say they want love and peace, they are instinctively aggressive toward each other.

As you read, consider the following questions:

1. Why does Freud believe there is a mutual hostility between people?
2. According to Freud, what principle will defeat the Communists' hope of building a cooperative society?
3. Does Freud view humans in only aggressive terms, or is there a positive side to human nature?

From *Civilization and Its Discontents*, by Sigmund Freud, in *The Standard Edition of the Complete Psychological Works of Sigmund Freud*, translated by James Strachey. Translation copyright ©1961 by James Strachey, renewed 1989 by Alix Strachey. Reprinted by permission of W.W. Norton and Company, Inc., The Hogarth Press, and The Institute of Psycho-Analysis.

The element of truth behind all this, which people are so ready to disavow, is that men are not gentle creatures who want to be loved, and who at the most can defend themselves if they are attacked; they are, on the contrary, creatures among whose instinctual endowments is to be reckoned a powerful share of aggressiveness. As a result, their neighbour is for them not only a potential helper or sexual object, but also someone who tempts them to satisfy their aggressiveness on him, to exploit his capacity for work without compensation, to use him sexually without his consent, to seize his possessions, to humiliate him, to cause him pain, to torture and to kill him. *Homo homini lupus.* ['Man is a wolf to man.'] Who, in the face of all his experience of life and of history, will have the courage to dispute this assertion? . . .

HUMANS ARE AGGRESSIVE

The existence of this inclination to aggression, which we can detect in ourselves and justly assume to be present in others, is the factor which disturbs our relations with our neighbour and which forces civilization into such a high expenditure [of energy]. In consequence of this primary mutual hostility of human beings, civilized society is perpetually threatened with disintegration. The interest of work in common would not hold it together; instinctual passions are stronger than reasonable interests. Civilization has to use its utmost efforts in order to set limits to man's aggressive instincts and to hold the manifestations of them in check by psychical reaction-formations. Hence, therefore, the use of methods intended to incite people into identifications and aim-inhibited relationships of love, hence the restriction upon sexual life, and hence too the ideal's commandment to love one's neighbour as oneself—a commandment which is really justified by the fact that nothing else runs so strongly counter to the original nature of man. In spite of every effort, these endeavours of civilization have not so far achieved very much. It hopes to prevent the crudest excesses of brutal violence by itself assuming the right to use violence against criminals, but the law is not able to lay hold of the more cautious and refined manifestations of human aggressiveness. The time comes when each one of us has to give up as illusions the expectations which, in his youth, he pinned upon his fellowmen, and when he may learn how much difficulty and pain has been added to his life by their ill-will. At the same time, it would be unfair to reproach civilization with trying to eliminate strife and competition from human activity. These things are undoubtedly indispensable. But opposition is not necessarily enmity; it is merely misused and made an *occasion* for enmity.

THE ENVIRONMENT DOES NOT CAUSE AGGRESSION

The communists believe that they have found the path to deliverance from our evils. According to them, man is wholly good and is well-disposed to his neighbour; but the institution of private property has corrupted his nature. The ownership of private wealth gives the individual power, and with it the temptation to ill-treat his neighbour; while the man who is excluded from possession is bound to rebel in hostility against his oppressor. If private property were abolished, all wealth held in common, and everyone allowed to share in the enjoyment of it, ill-will and hostility would disappear among men. Since everyone's needs would be satisfied, no one would have any reason to regard another as his enemy; all would willingly undertake the work that was necessary. I have no concern with any economic criticisms of the communist system; I cannot enquire into whether the abolition of private property is expedient or advantageous. But I am able to recognize that the psychological premises on which the system is based are an untenable illusion. In abolishing private property we deprive the human love of aggression of one of its instruments, certainly a strong one, though certainly not the strongest; but we have in no way altered the differences in power and influence which are misused by aggressiveness, nor have we altered anything in its nature. Aggressiveness was not created by property. It reigned almost without limit in primitive times, when property was still very scanty, and it already shows itself in the nursery almost before property has given up its primal, anal form; it forms the basis of every relation of affection and love among people (with the single exception, perhaps, of the mother's relation to her male child). If we do away with personal rights over material wealth, there still remains prerogative in the field of sexual relationships, which is bound to become the source of the strongest dislike and the most violent hostility among men who in other respects are on an equal footing. If we were to remove this factor, too, by allowing complete freedom of sexual life and thus abolishing the family, the germ-cell of civilization, we cannot, it is true, easily foresee what new paths the development of civilization could take; but one thing we can expect, and that is that this indestructible feature of human nature will follow it there.

It is clearly not easy for men to give up the satisfaction of this inclination to aggression. They do not feel comfortable without it. The advantage which a comparatively small cultural group offers of allowing this instinct an outlet in the form of hostility against intruders is not to be despised. It is always possible to bind together a considerable number of people in love, so long as there are other people left over to receive the manifestations of their aggressiveness. I once discussed the phenomenon that it is precisely communities with adjoining territories, and related to each other in other ways as well, who are engaged in constant feuds and in ridiculing each other—like the Spaniards and Portuguese, for instance, the North Germans and South Germans, the English and Scotch, and so on. I gave this phenomenon the name of 'the narcissism of minor differences', a name which does not do much to explain it. We can now see that it is a convenient and relatively harmless satisfaction of the inclination to aggression, by means of which cohesion between the members of the community is made easier. In this respect the Jewish people, scattered everywhere, have rendered most useful services to the civilizations of the countries that have been their hosts. . . .

HUMAN NATURE IS DIVIDED
In all that follows I adopt the standpoint, therefore, that the inclination to aggression is an original, self-subsisting instinctual disposition in man, and I return to my view that it constitutes the greatest impediment to civilization. At one point in the

course of this enquiry I was led to the idea that civilization was a special process which mankind undergoes, and I am still under the influence of that idea. I may now add that civilization is a process in the service of Eros, whose purpose is to combine single human individuals, and after that families, then races, peoples and nations, into one great unity, the unity of mankind. Why this has to happen, we do not know; the work of Eros is precisely this. These collections of men are to be libidinally bound to one another. Necessity alone, the advantages of work in common, will not hold them together. But man's natural aggressive instinct, the hostility of each against all and of all against each, opposes this programme of civilization. This aggressive instinct is the derivative and the main representative of the death instinct which we have found alongside of Eros and which shares world-dominion with it. And now, I think, the meaning of the evolution of civilization is no longer obscure to us. It must present the struggle between Eros and Death, between the instinct of life and the instinct of destruction, as it works itself out in the human species. This struggle is what all life essentially consists of, and the evolution of civilization may therefore be simply described as the struggle for life of the human species. And it is this battle of the giants that our nursemaids try to appease with their lullaby about Heaven.

> "The Chalice and the Blade *tells a new story of our cultural origins. It shows that war and the 'war of the sexes' are neither divinely nor biologically ordained."*

HUMAN NATURE IS NOT AGGRESSIVE

Riane Eisler

Sigmund Freud assumes that it is impossible to remove the aggressive tendencies of human nature. Riane Eisler strongly disagrees with the idea that humans have only one way of relating to each other. She believes that social structures, not human nature, determine whether people are aggressive. While admitting that in the past, humans have evolved aggressively, Eisler is hopeful that the future direction of human social evolution can be changed. According to Eisler, cooperation, rather than competition, can be established between the genders and between peoples. Eisler, who escaped Nazi-occupied Austria as a child, promotes a new model of human relationships and self-understanding, which she calls "partnership."

As you read, consider the following questions:

1. What does Eisler mean by the "dominator model" and the "partnership model"?
2. According to the author, what was "the original direction in the mainstream of our cultural evolution"?
3. According to Eisler, what changed the original direction of human societies?

Why do we hunt and persecute each other? Why is our world so full of man's infamous inhumanity to man—and to woman? How can human beings be so brutal to their own kind? What is it that chronically tilts us toward cruelty rather than kindness, toward war rather than peace, toward destruction rather than actualization?

Of all life-forms on this planet, only we can plant and harvest fields, compose poetry and music, seek truth and justice, teach a child to read and write—or even laugh and cry. Because of our unique ability to imagine new realities and realize these through ever more advanced technologies, we are quite literally partners in our own evolution. And yet, this same wondrous species of ours now seems bent on putting an end not only to its own evolution but to that of most life on our globe, threatening our planet with ecological catastrophe or nuclear annihilation.

EVOLUTIONARY CROSSROADS

As time went on, as I pursued my professional studies, had children, and increasingly focused my research and writing on the future, my concerns broadened and deepened. Like many people, I became convinced that we are rapidly approaching an evolutionary crossroads—that never before has the course we choose been so critical. But what course should we take?

Socialists and communists assert that the root of our problems is capitalism; capitalists insist socialism and communism are leading us to ruin. Some argue our troubles are due to our "industrial paradigm," that our "scientific worldview" is to blame. Still others blame humanism, feminism, and even secularism, pressing for a return to the "good old days" of a smaller, simpler, more religious age.

Yet, if we look at ourselves—as we are forced to by television or the grim daily ritual of the newspaper at breakfast—we see how capitalist, socialist, and communist nations alike are enmeshed in the arms race and all the other irrationalities that threaten both us and our environment. And if we look at our past—at the routine massacres by Huns, Romans, Vikings, and Assyrians or the cruel slaughters of the Christian Crusades and Inquisition—we see there was even more violence and injustice in the smaller, prescientific, preindustrial societies that came before us.

Since going backward is not the answer, how do we move forward? A great deal is being written about a New Age, a major and unprecedented cultural transformation. But in practical terms, what does this mean? A transformation from what to what? In terms of both our everyday lives and our cultural evolution, what precisely would be different, or even possible, in the future? Is a shift from a system leading to chronic wars, social injustice, and ecological imbalance to one of peace, social justice, and ecological balance a realistic possibility? Most important, what changes in social structure would make such a transformation possible?

LOOKING FOR NEW ANSWERS

The search for answers to these questions led me to the reexamination of our past, present, and future on which this book is based. *The Chalice and the Blade* reports part of this new study of human society, which differs from most prior studies in that it takes into account the *whole* of human history (including our prehistory) as well as the *whole* of humanity (both its female and male halves).

LONGING FOR THE LOST PAST

I believe man once lived in utopia, but does no longer, and that he is always trying to return. The name of his first utopia was Eden. I do not care whether one conceives of Eden as a tract of real estate or a purely metaphysical garden. It may never have existed 'in time'. But, however conceived, it is a part of our heritage. We want to go back. The flaming swords of angels bar the way. So we must create another garden, a new Eden.

We are haunted by memories of the original garden and that lost innocence. In our heart of hearts, we know that our race has not always lived in the world of historical time, a world shot through with oppression, misunderstanding, meaningless tragedy, cruelty, individual and collective insanity; a world only haphazardly redeemed by some moments and deeds of niggardly virtue and grudging magnanimity, and fugitive instants of compassion and love. It was not always so. Metaphysically if not historically, it was not always so. The poor thing we commonly call our 'human nature' was not our first nature; it is a pathological condition.

Chad Walsh, From Utopia to Nightmare, 1962.

Weaving together evidence from art, archaeology, religion, social science, history, and many other fields of inquiry into new patterns that more accurately fit the best available data, *The Chalice and the Blade* tells a new story of our cultural origins. It shows that war and the "war of the sexes" are neither divinely nor biologically ordained. And it provides verification that a better future is possible—and is in fact firmly rooted in the haunting drama of what actually happened in our past. . . .

One result of re-examining human society from a gender-holistic perspective has been a new theory of cultural evolution. This theory, which I have called Cultural Transformation theory, proposes that underlying the great surface diversity of human culture are two basic models of society.

The first, which I call the *dominator* model, is what is popularly termed either patriarchy or matriarchy—the *ranking* of one half of humanity over the other. The second, in which social rela-tions are primarily based on the principle of *linking* rather than ranking, may best be described as the *partnership* model. In this model—beginning with the most fundamental difference in our species, between male and female—diversity is not equated with either inferiority or superiority.

ORIGINAL DIRECTION OF CULTURAL EVOLUTION

Cultural Transformation theory further proposes that the original direction in the mainstream of our cultural evolution was toward partnership but that, following a period of chaos and almost to-tal cultural disruption, there occurred a fundamental social shift. The greater availability of data on Western societies (due to the ethnocentric focus of Western social science) makes it possible to document this shift in more detail through the analysis of West-ern cultural evolution. However, there are also indications that this change in direction from a partnership to a dominator model was roughly paralleled in other parts of the world.

The title *The Chalice and the Blade* derives from this cataclysmic turning point during the prehistory of Western civilization, when the direction of our cultural evolution was quite literally turned around. At this pivotal branching, the cultural evolution of societies that worshiped the life-generating and nurturing powers of the universe—in our time still symbolized by the an-cient chalice or grail—was interrupted. There now appeared on the prehistoric horizon invaders from the peripheral areas of our globe who ushered in a very different form of social organi-zation. As the University of California archaeologist Marija Gimbutas writes, these were people who worshiped "the lethal power of the blade"—the power to take rather than give life that is the ultimate power to establish and enforce domination.

Today we stand at another potentially decisive branching point. At a time when the lethal power of the Blade—amplified a millionfold by megatons of nuclear warheads—threatens to put an end to all human culture, the new findings about both ancient and modern history reported in *The Chalice and the Blade* do not merely provide a new chapter in the story of our past. Of greatest importance is what this new knowledge tells us about our present and potential future.

Aggression Is Not Inevitable

For millennia men have fought wars and the Blade has been a male symbol. But this does not mean men are inevitably violent and warlike. Throughout recorded history there have been peaceful and nonviolent men. Moreover, obviously there were both men and women in the prehistoric societies where the power to give and nurture, which the Chalice symbolizes, was supreme. The underlying problem is not men as a sex. The root of the problem lies in a social system in which the power of the Blade is idealized—in which both men and women are taught to equate true masculinity with violence and dominance and to see men who do not conform to this ideal as "too soft" or "effeminate."

Lessons from Genesis

With good cause, therefore, does the true religion recognise and proclaim that the same God who created the universal cosmos, created also all the animals, souls as well as bodies. Among the terrestrial animals man was made by Him in His own image, and, for the reason I have given, was made one individual, though he was not left solitary. For there is nothing so social by nature, so unsocial by its corruption, as this race. And human nature has nothing more appropriate, either for the prevention of discord, or for the healing of it, where it exists, than the remembrance of that first parent of us all, whom God was pleased to create alone, that all men might be derived from one, and that they might thus be admonished to preserve unity among their whole multitude. But from the fact that the woman was made for him from his side, it was plainly meant that we should learn how dear the bond between man and wife should be.

Saint Augustine, *The City of God*, 426.

For many people it is difficult to believe that any other way of structuring human society is possible—much less that our future may hinge on anything connected with women or femininity. One reason for these beliefs is that in male-dominant societies anything associated with women or femininity is automatically viewed as a secondary, or women's, issue—to be addressed, if at all, only after the "more important" problems have been resolved. Another reason is that we have not had the necessary information. Even though humanity obviously consists of two halves (women and men), in most studies of human society the main protagonist, indeed often the sole actor, has been male.

As a result of what has been quite literally "the study of man," most social scientists have had to work with such an incomplete and distorted data base that in any other context it would immediately have been recognized as deeply flawed. Even now, information about women is primarily relegated to the intellectual ghetto of women's studies. Moreover, and quite understandably because of its immediate (though long neglected) importance for the lives of women, most research by feminists has focused on the implications of the study of women for women.

This book is different in that it focuses on the implications of how we organize the relations between the two halves of humanity for the totality of a social system. Clearly, how these relations are structured has decisive implications for the personal lives of both men and women, for our day-to-day roles and life options. But equally important, although still generally ignored, is something that once articulated seems obvious. This is that the way we structure the most fundamental of all human relations (without which our species could not go on) has a profound effect on every one of our institutions, on our values, and . . . on the direction of our cultural evolution, particularly whether it will be peaceful or warlike.

"The man and his wife were both naked, and they felt no shame."

HUMAN NATURE WAS CORRUPTED BY SIN

Genesis

The Old Testament gives a rather simple description of human origins. "Man," who is described as both male and female, is created in the image of God. Further, "man" is created from both the dust of the earth and the breath of God. This passage has been interpreted by many to point to a fundamental division; humans are a mixture of physical and spiritual qualities. Genesis presents Adam as incomplete without Eve. The ideal state of humanity, in contrast to Rousseau, is not the lone individual. Later, Eve is tempted to gain wisdom and Cain is tempted to kill his brother. Writers have used these accounts to conclude that humans are dissatisfied, longing for things which are not really good for them. The nakedness of Adam and Eve suggests innocence and security. When this innocence and security are lost, garments are required to hide this loss. It is also interesting to note how Cain's dilemma is described. He is divided. God tells him to make a choice between submitting to sin or mastering sin. These stories in Genesis have provided many people with an outline to develop their understanding of human nature.

As you read, consider the following questions:

1. How would you interpret the phrase "made in the image of God"?
2. Why is Adam told to give names to the animals in the garden?
3. The Garden of Eden is presented as a fruitful and beautiful place. What causes Adam and Eve to be expelled from the garden?

From Genesis 1:1–5, 24–2:1, 2:7–4:16, New International Version.

In the beginning God created the heavens and the earth. Now the earth was formless and empty, darkness was over the surface of the deep, and the Spirit of God was hovering over the waters.

THE FIRST DAY OF CREATION

And God said, "Let there be light," and there was light. God saw that the light was good, and he separated the light from the darkness. God called the light "day," and the darkness he called "night." And there was evening, and there was morning—the first day. . . .

THE SIXTH DAY OF CREATION

And God said, "Let the land produce living creatures according to their kinds: livestock, creatures that move along the ground, and wild animals, each according to its kind." And it was so. God made the wild animals according to their kinds, the livestock according to their kinds, and all the creatures that move along the ground according to their kinds. And God saw that it was good.

IN THE IMAGE OF GOD

Then God said, "Let us make man in our image, in our likeness, and let them rule over the fish of the sea and the birds of the air, over the livestock, over all the earth, and over all the creatures that move along the ground."

So God created man in his own image, in the image of God he created him; male and female he created them.

God blessed them and said to them, "Be fruitful and increase in number; fill the earth and subdue it. Rule over the fish of the sea and the birds of the air and over every living creature that moves on the ground."

Then God said, "I give you every seed-bearing plant on the face of the whole earth and every tree that has fruit with seed in it. They will be yours for food. And to all the beasts of the earth and all the birds of the air and all the creatures that move on the ground—everything that has the breath of life in it—I give every green plant for food." And it was so.

God saw all that he had made, and it was very good. And there was evening, and there was morning—the sixth day.

Thus the heavens and the earth were completed in all their vast array. . . .

The LORD God formed the man from the dust of the ground and breathed into his nostrils the breath of life, and the man became a living being.

Now the LORD God had planted a garden in the east, in Eden; and there he put the man he had formed. And the LORD God made all kinds of trees grow out of the ground—trees that were pleasing to eye and good for food. In the middle of the garden were the tree of life and the tree of the knowledge of good and evil.

A river watering the garden flowed from Eden; from there it was separated into four headwaters. The name of the first is the Pishon; it winds through the entire land of Havilah, where there is gold. (The gold of that land is good; aromatic resin and onyx are also there.) The name of the second river is the Gihon; it winds through the entire land of Cush. The name of the third river is the Tigris; it runs along the east side of Asshur. And the fourth river is the Euphrates.

TREE OF GOOD AND EVIL

The LORD God took the man and put him in the Garden of Eden to work it and take care of it. And the LORD God commanded the man, "You are free to eat from any tree in the garden; but you must not eat from the tree of the knowledge of good and evil, for when you eat of it you will surely die."

ADAM IS NO LONGER ALONE

The LORD God said, "It is not good for the man to be alone. I will make a helper suitable for him."

Now the LORD God had formed out of the ground all the beasts of the field and all the birds of the air. He brought them to the man to see what he would name them; and whatever the man called each living creature, that was its name. So the man gave names to all the livestock, the birds of the air and all the beasts of the field.

But for Adam no suitable helper was found. So the LORD God caused the man to fall into a deep sleep; and while he was sleeping, he took one of the man's ribs and closed up the place with flesh. Then the LORD God made a woman from the rib he had taken out of the man, and he brought her to the man.

The man said,

"This is now bone of my bones
    and flesh of my flesh;
she shall be called 'woman,'
    for she was taken out of
    man."

For this reason a man will leave his father and mother and be united to his wife, and they will become one flesh.

The man and his wife were both naked, and they felt no shame.

Now the serpent was more crafty than any of the wild animals the LORD God had made. He said to the woman, "Did God really say, 'You must not eat from any tree in the garden'?"

The woman said to the serpent, "We may eat fruit from the trees in the garden, but God did say, 'You must not eat fruit from the tree that is in the middle of the garden, and you must not touch it, or you will die.'"

"You will not surely die," the serpent said to the woman. "For God knows that when you eat of it your eyes will be opened, and you will be like God, knowing good and evil."

When the woman saw that the fruit of the tree was good for food and pleasing to the eye, and also desirable for gaining wisdom, she took some and ate it. She also gave some to her husband, who was with her, and he ate it.

BROKEN RELATIONSHIPS

Then the eyes of both of them were opened, and they realized they were naked; so they sewed fig leaves together and made coverings for themselves.

Then the man and his wife heard the sound of the LORD God as he was walking in the garden in the cool of the day, and they hid from the LORD God among the trees of the garden. But the LORD God called to the man, "Where are you?"

He answered, "I heard you in the garden, and I was afraid because I was naked; so I hid."

And he said, "Who told you that you were naked? Have you eaten from the tree that I commanded you not to eat from?"

The man said, "The woman you put here with me—she gave me some fruit from the tree, and I ate it."

Then the LORD God said to the woman, "What is this you have done?"

The woman said, "The serpent deceived me, and I ate."

JUDGMENT FOR SIN

So the LORD God said to the serpent, "Because you have done this,

"Cursed are you above all the
    livestock
  and all the wild animals!
You will crawl on your belly
  and you will eat dust
  all the days of your life.
And I will put enmity
  between you and the woman,

and between your offspring
    and hers;
he will crush your head,
    and you will strike his heel."

To the woman he said,

"I will greatly increase your
    pains in childbearing;
    with pain you will give birth
    to children.
Your desire will be for your
    husband,
    and he will rule over you."

To Adam he said, "Because you listened to your wife and ate from the tree about which I commanded you, 'You must not eat of it,'

"Cursed is the ground because
    of you;
    through painful toil you will
    eat of it all the days of your life.
It will produce thorns and
    thistles for you,
    and you will eat the plants of
    the field.
By the sweat of your brow
  you will eat your food
until you return to the ground,
    since from it you were taken;
for dust you are
    and to dust you will return."

Adam named his wife Eve, because she would become the mother of all the living.

Loss of Eden

The LORD God made garments of skin for Adam and his wife and clothed them. And the LORD God said, "The man has now become like one of us, knowing good and evil. He must not be allowed to reach out his hand and take also from the tree of life and eat, and live forever." So the LORD God banished him from the Garden of Eden to work the ground from which he had been taken. After he drove the man out, he placed on the east side of the Garden of Eden cherubim and a flaming sword flashing back and forth to guard the way to the tree of life.

Adam lay with his wife Eve, and she became pregnant and gave birth to Cain. She said, "With the help of the LORD I have brought forth a man." Later she gave birth to his brother Abel.

Now Abel kept flocks, and Cain worked the soil. In the course of time Cain brought some of the fruits of the soil as an offering to the LORD. But Abel brought fat portions from some of the firstborn of his flock. The LORD looked with favor on Abel and his offering, but on Cain and his offering he did not look with favor. So Cain was very angry, and his face was downcast.

Then the LORD said to Cain, "Why are you angry? Why is your face downcast? If you do what is right, will you not be accepted? But if you do not do what is right, sin is crouching at your door; it desires to have you, but you must master it."

Now Cain said to his brother Abel, "Let's go out to the field." And while they were in the field, Cain attacked his brother Abel and killed him.

Then the LORD said to Cain, "Where is your brother Abel?"

"I don't know," he replied. "Am I my brother's keeper?"

The LORD said, "What have you done? Listen! Your brother's blood cries out to me from the ground. Now you are under a curse and driven from the ground, which opened its mouth to receive your brother's blood from your hand. When you work the ground, it will no longer yield its crops for you. You will be a restless wanderer on the earth."

Cain said to the LORD, "My punishment is more than I can bear. Today you are driving me from the land, and I will be hidden from your presence; I will be a restless wanderer on the earth, and whoever finds me will kill me."

But the LORD said to him, "Not so; if anyone kills Cain, he will suffer vengeance seven times over." Then the LORD put a mark on Cain so that no one who found him would kill him. So Cain went out from the LORD's presence and lived in the land of Nod, east of Eden.

"Man still bears in his bodily frame
the indelible stamp of his lowly
origin."

HUMAN NATURE IS AN EXTENSION
OF ANIMAL EVOLUTION

Charles Darwin

The idea that humans have evolved from animals can give
people a sense of pride or humiliation, or both. Charles Darwin
(1809–1882) was not the first person to propose the idea of
evolution. He was, however, the first to successfully develop an
explanation of how such development might take place across
the various species, particularly from animals to humans. Darwin concludes that humans are not significantly different from
the "lower life forms."

As you read, consider the following questions:

1. According to Darwin, what "higher" qualities in humans
   have evolved by natural selection?
2. What physical similarities between humans and other
   mammals does Darwin point out?
3. According to the author, why do humans feel pride and
   humbleness in their ancestry?

From the General Summary and Conclusion of The Descent of Man, by Charles Darwin
(New York: Collier, 1902).

The main conclusion here arrived at, and now held by many naturalists who are well competent to form a sound judgment, is that man is descended from some less highly organised form. The grounds upon which this conclusion rests will never be shaken, for the close similarity between man and the lower animals in embryonic development, as well as in innumerable points of structure and constitution, both of high and of the most trifling importance,—the rudiments which he retains, and the abnormal reversions to which he is occasionally liable,—are facts which cannot be disputed. They have long been known, but until recently they told us nothing with respect to the origin of man. Now when viewed by the light of our knowledge of the whole organic world, their meaning is unmistakable. The great principle of evolution stands up clear and firm, when these groups or facts are considered in connection with others, such as the mutual affinities of the members of the same group, their geographical distribution in past and present times, and their geological succession. It is incredible that all these facts should speak falsely. He who is not content to look, like a savage, at the phenomena of nature as disconnected, cannot any longer believe that man is the work of a separate act of creation. He will be forced to admit that the close resemblance of the embryo of man to that, for instance, of a dog—the construction of his skull, limbs and whole frame on the same plan with that of other mammals, independently of the uses to which the parts may be put—the occasional re-appearance of various structures, for instance of several muscles, which man does not normally possess, but which are common to the Quadrumana [literally, "four-handed" primates]—and a crowd of analogous facts—all point in the plainest manner to the conclusion that man is the co-descendant with other mammals of a common progenitor.

We have seen that man incessantly presents individual differences in all parts of his body and in his mental faculties. These differences or variations seem to be induced by the same general causes, and to obey the same laws as with the lower animals. In both cases similar laws of inheritance prevail. . . .

INTELLECTUAL DEVELOPMENT

The high standard of our intellectual powers and moral disposition is the greatest difficulty which presents itself, after we have been driven to this conclusion on the origin of man. But every one who admits the principle of evolution, must see that the mental powers of the higher animals, which are the same in kind with those of man, though so different in degree, are capable of

78

advancement. Thus the interval between the mental powers of one of the higher apes and of a fish, or between those of an ant and scale-insect, is immense; yet their development does not offer any special difficulty; for with our domesticated animals, the mental faculties are certainly variable, and the variations are inherited. No one doubts that they are of the utmost importance to animals in a state of nature. Therefore the conditions are favourable for their development through natural selection. The same conclusion may be extended to man; the intellect must have been all-important to him, even at a very remote period, as enabling him to invent and use language, to make weapons, tools, traps, &c., whereby with the aid of his social habits, he long ago became the most dominant of all living creatures.

THE ROLE OF LANGUAGE

A great stride in the development of the intellect will have followed, as soon as the half-art and half-instinct of language came into use; for the continued use of language will have reacted on the brain and produced an inherited effect; and this again will have reacted on the improvement of language. As Mr. Chauncey Wright has well remarked, the largeness of the brain in man relatively to his body, compared with the lower animals, may be attributed in chief part to the early use of some simple form of language,—that wonderful engine which affixes signs to all sorts of objects and qualities, and excites trains of thought which would never arise from the mere impression of the senses, or if they did arise could not be followed out. The higher intellectual powers of man, such as those of ratiocination, abstraction, self-consciousness, &c., probably follow from the continued improvement and exercise of the other mental faculties.

MORAL DEVELOPMENT

The development of the moral qualities is a more interesting problem. The foundation lies in the social instincts, including under this term the family ties. These instincts are highly complex, and in the case of the lower animals give special tendencies towards certain definite actions; but the more important elements are love, and the distinct emotion of sympathy. Animals endowed with the social instincts take pleasure in one another's company, warn one another of danger, defend and aid one another in many ways. These instincts do not extend to all the individuals of the species, but only to those of the same community. As they are highly beneficial to the species, they have in all probability been acquired through natural selection. . . .

Man scans with scrupulous care the character and pedigree of his horses, cattle, and dogs before he matches them; but when he comes to his own marriage he rarely, or never, takes any such care. He is impelled by nearly the same motives as the lower animals, when they are left to their own free choice, though he is in so far superior to them that he highly values mental charms and virtues. On the other hand he is strongly attracted by mere wealth or rank. Yet he might by selection do something not only for the bodily constitution and frame of his offspring, but for their intellectual and moral qualities. Both sexes ought to refrain from marriage if they are in any marked degree inferior in body or mind; but such hopes are Utopian and will never be even partially realised until the laws of inheritance are thoroughly known. Everyone does good service, who aids towards this end. When the principles of breeding and inheritance are better understood, we shall not hear ignorant members of our legislature rejecting with scorn a plan for ascertaining whether or not consanguineous marriages are injurious to man.

THE STRUGGLE FOR EXISTENCE

Darwin's expression, "the struggle for existence," is sometimes erroneously interpreted as the struggle between different species. In reality, the struggle Darwin was thinking of and which drives evolution forward is the competition between near relations. What causes a species to disappear or become transformed into a different species is the profitable "invention" that falls by chance to one or a few of its members in the everlasting gamble of hereditary change. The descendants of these lucky ones gradually outstrip all others until the particular species consists only of individuals who possess the new "invention."

Konrad Lorenz, On Aggression, 1963.

The advancement of the welfare of mankind is a most intricate problem: all ought to refrain from marriage who cannot avoid abject poverty for their children; for poverty is not only a great evil, but tends to its own increase by leading to recklessness in marriage. On the other hand, as Mr. Galton has remarked, if the prudent avoid marriage, whilst the reckless marry, the inferior members tend to supplant the better members of society. Man, like every other animal, has no doubt advanced to his present high condition through a struggle for existence consequent on his rapid multiplication; and if he is to advance still higher, it is to be feared that he must remain subject to a severe struggle. Otherwise he would sink into indolence, and the more gifted men would not be more successful in the battle of life than the less gifted. Hence our natural rate of increase though leading to many and obvious evils must not be greatly diminished by any means. There should be open competition for all men; and the most able should not be prevented by laws or customs from succeeding best and rearing the largest number of offspring. Important as the struggle for existence has been and even still is, yet as far as the highest part of man's nature is concerned there are other agencies more important. For the moral qualities are advanced, either directly or indirectly, much more through the effects of habit, the reasoning powers, instruction, religion, &c., than through natural selection; though to this latter agency may be safely attributed the social instincts, which afforded the basis for the development of the moral sense.

Our Ancestors

The main conclusion arrived at in this work, namely, that man is descended from some lowly organised form, will, I regret to think, be highly distasteful to many. But there can hardly be a doubt that we are descended from barbarians. The astonishment which I felt on first seeing a party of Fuegians on a wild and broken shore will never be forgotten by me, for the reflection at once rushed into my mind—such were our ancestors. These men were absolutely naked and bedaubed with paint, their long hair was tangled, their mouths frothed with excitement, and their expression was wild, startled, and distrustful. They possessed hardly any arts, and like wild animals lived on what they could catch; they had no government, and were merciless to every one not of their own small tribe. He who has seen a savage in his native land will not feel much shame, if forced to acknowledge that the blood of some more humble creature flows in his veins. For my own part I would as soon be descended from that heroic little monkey, who braved his dreaded enemy in order to save the life of his keeper, or from that old baboon, who descending from the mountains, carried away in triumph his young comrade from a crowd of astonished dogs—as from a savage who delights to torture his enemies, offers up bloody sacrifices, practices infanticide without remorse, treats his wives like slaves, knows no decency, and is haunted by the grossest superstitions.

Pride and Humility

Man may be excused for feeling some pride at having risen, though not through his own exertions, to the very summit of the organic scale; and the fact of his having thus risen, instead of having been aboriginally placed there, may give him hope for a still higher destiny in the distant future. But we are not here concerned with hopes or fears, only with the truth as far as our reason permits us to discover it; and I have given the evidence to the best of my ability. We must, however, acknowledge, as it seems to me, that man with all his noble qualities, with sympathy which feels for the most debased, with benevolence which extends not only to other men but to the humblest living creature, with his god-like intellect which has penetrated into the movements and constitution of the solar system—with all these exalted powers—Man still bears in his bodily frame the indelible stamp of his lowly origin.

CHAPTER 3

WHAT CAUSES HUMAN CONFLICTS?

CHAPTER PREFACE

French mathematician and theologian Blaise Pascal represents a number of writers who see deep conflicts built into the nature of humanity. Pascal views human nature as a puzzle that does not fit together. For example, Pascal writes, humans are physically weak, yet they can transcend that weakness with their reason and spirit. Pascal concludes that human nature exists, but he finds it so filled with contradictions that it is impossible to fully understand.

The biblical apostle Paul also refers to the conflicts found within human nature. However, Paul focuses on a raging conflict between humanity and God. Paul writes that it is natural for humans to be at odds with their creator and to actively suppress their awareness of God. As a result, God gave them over to sinful, self-destructive behavior.

The nineteenth-century writer Washington Irving represents another perspective on human life. He observes that the fundamental conflict in human experience is an inability to live at peace with nature, with others, and with one's self. Irving explains that "civilized" whites have lost a simplicity, innocence, and harmony in their lives. In contrast, he contends that the Native Americans encountered in the unsettled plains are at peace with nature and with themselves.

Conflicts between women and men date back to the dawn of civilization. Writer and political activist Simone de Beauvoir writes that gender conflicts are rooted in social forces. While admitting minor biological differences, de Beauvoir is concerned about those social habits that create friction between males and females. Such friction is not a part of human nature and is, therefore, not inevitable.

Deborah Tannen looks at the actual behavior of adults and finds differences in how females and males communicate. Tannen explains that these differences, whether caused by genetics or social training, need to be understood if males and females want to reduce their conflicts.

| "There is internal war in man between reason and the passions. . . . He is always divided against and opposed to himself."

HUMANS ARE IN CONFLICT WITHIN THEMSELVES

Blaise Pascal

Blaise Pascal (1623–1662) was a genius in math and science. He was also a spiritually sensitive Christian layman. Though he was a man of great intellect, he constantly reminds his audience of the limitations of our knowledge. For example, Pascal repeatedly states that the things which are most important to know, such as the nature of God and the nature of humanity, are far beyond our mental grasp. His *Pensées* is a collection of rambling ideas which he had planned to make into a book. The passages below show how Pascal viewed human nature as paradoxical.

As you read, consider the following questions:

1. According to Pascal, what makes humans special?
2. Why does Pascal call man "an incomprehensible monster"?
3. What does the author say about the inner conversations an individual has with himself or herself?

From Blaise Pascal, *Pensées*, sections 6 and 7, translated by W.F. Trotter, (London: J. M. Dent, 1919).

347. Man is but a reed, the most feeble thing in nature; but he is a thinking reed. The entire universe need not arm itself to crush him. A vapour, a drop of water suffices to kill him. But, if the universe were to crush him, man would still be more noble than that which killed him, because he knows that he dies and the advantage which the universe has over him; the universe knows nothing of this.

All our dignity consists, then, in thought. By it we must elevate ourselves, and not by space and time which we cannot fill. Let us endeavour, then, to think well; this is the principle of morality.

348. *A thinking reed.*—It is not from space that I must seek my dignity, but from the government of my thought. I shall have no more if I possess worlds. By space the universe encompasses and swallows me up like an atom; by thought I comprehend the world. . . .

HUMAN GREATNESS, HUMAN WEAKNESS

397. The greatness of man is great in that he knows himself to be miserable. A tree does not know itself to be miserable. It is then being miserable to know oneself to be miserable; but it is also being great to know that one is miserable.

398. All these same miseries prove man's greatness. They are the miseries of a great lord, of a deposed king.

399. We are not miserable without feeling it. A ruined house is not miserable. Man only is miserable. *Ego vir videns.* [I am the man who has seen.]

400. *The greatness of man.*—We have so great an idea of the soul of man that we cannot endure being despised, or not being esteemed by any soul; and all the happiness of men consists in this esteem. . . .

409. *The greatness of man.*—The greatness of man is so evident that it is even proved by his wretchedness. For what in animals is *nature*, we call in man *wretchedness*; by which we recognise that, his nature being now like that of animals, he has fallen from a better nature which once was his. . . .

AN INNER WAR

412. There is internal war in man between reason and the passions.

If he had only reason without passions . . .

If he had only passions without reason . . .

But having both, he cannot be without strife, being unable to be at peace with the one without being at war with the other. Thus he is always divided against and opposed to himself.

413. This internal war of reason against the passions has made a division of those who would have peace into two sects. The first would renounce their passions and become gods; the others would renounce reason and become brute beasts. ([French poet Jacques] Des Barreaux.) But neither can do so, and reason still remains, to condemn the vileness and injustice of the passions and to trouble the repose of those who abandon themselves to them; and the passions keep always alive in those who would renounce them.

414. Men are so necessarily mad that not to be mad would amount to another form of madness. . . .

An Incomprehensible Monster

420. If he exalt himself, I humble him; if he humble himself, I exalt him; and I always contradict him, till he understands that he is an incomprehensible monster.

421. I blame equally those who choose to praise man, those who choose to blame him, and those who choose to amuse themselves; and I can only approve of those who seek with lamentation.

422. It is good to be tired and wearied by the vain search after the true good, that we may stretch out our arms to the Redeemer.

Contradictions in Human Nature

The real enigma of man is the conflict within his own nature, not the fact that he is composed of body and soul; the real problem does not lie in the fact that man is part of the world and is yet more than the world; the real problem is that the unity of all these elements—given by the Creation—has been lost, and that instead of complementing and aiding one another, they are in conflict with one another. Non-Christian anthropology tries to deal with this conflict in two ways: either by ascribing it to the constitutional conflict between sense and spirit, or it seeks to resolve the discord by suggesting that the difficulties are merely successive phases in a process of development, continuous stages in self-realization. The Christian doctrine takes this conflict seriously: man, by his own act of self-determination, contradicts the divine determination in the Creation. It is this duality which gives its particular imprint to human life as it actually is. Because man has been created in the image of God, and yet has himself defaced this image, his existence differs from all other forms of existence, as existence in conflict.

Emil Brunner, *Man in Revolt*, 1939.

423. *Contraries. After having shown the vileness and the greatness of man.*—Let man now know his value. Let him love himself, for there is in him a nature capable of good; but let him not for this reason love the vileness which is in him. Let him despise himself, for this capacity is barren; but let him not therefore despise this natural capacity. Let him hate himself, let him love himself; he has within him the capacity of knowing the truth and of being happy, but he possesses no truth, either constant or satisfactory.

I would then lead man to the desire of finding truth; to be free from passions, and ready to follow it where he may find it, knowing how much his knowledge is obscured by the passions. I would, indeed, that he should hate in himself the lust which determined his will by itself so that it may not blind him in making his choice, and may not hinder him when he has chosen.

424. All these contradictions, which seem most to keep me from the knowledge of religion, have led me most quickly to the true one. . . .

GREATNESS AND WRETCHEDNESS

430. *For Port-Royal. The beginning, after having explained the incomprehensibility.*—The greatness and the wretchedness of man are so evident that the true religion must necessarily teach us both that there is in man some great source of greatness and a great source of wretchedness. It must then give us a reason for these astonishing contradictions. . . .

534. There are only two kinds of men: the righteous who believe themselves sinners; the rest, sinners, who believe themselves righteous. . . .

536. Man is so made that by continually telling him he is a fool he believes it, and by continually telling it to himself he makes himself believe it. For man holds an inward talk with his self alone, which it behoves him to regulate well: *Corrumpunt bonos mores colloquia prava.* [Evil communications corrupt good manners.] We must keep silent as much as possible and talk with ourselves only of God, whom we know to be true; and thus we convince ourselves of the truth.

"For although they knew God, they
neither glorified him as God nor
gave thanks to him, but their
thinking became futile and their
foolish hearts were darkened.
Although they claimed to be wise,
they became fools."

HUMANS ARE IN CONFLICT WITH GOD

Apostle Paul

Christian explanations of human nature have deeply influenced
Western thought and culture. One of the most important sources
of Christian doctrine has been the Apostle Paul's letter to the Roman church. Because Paul had not yet visited that church, he did
not write about particular issues, as in his other letters. In the
letter to the Romans, Paul gives a sweeping overview of early
Christian teachings. The selection below gives a brief look into
Paul's understanding of human nature, particularly into the con-
tinuing conflict between human nature and God. Paul's argument is that this conflict between humanity and God is the basis
for the conflicts between humans.

As you read, consider the following questions:

1. According to Paul, what is the natural response of humanity
   toward God?
2. What does Paul write about judging others?
3. What is Paul's response to those who divide the world
   between the people who claim to know the truth and those
   accused of not knowing the truth?

From Romans 1:13–2:24, 3:9–23, New International Version.

I do not want you to be unaware, brothers, that I planned many times to come to you (but have been prevented from doing so until now) in order that I might have a harvest among you, just as I have had among the other Gentiles.

I am obligated both to Greeks and non-Greeks, both to the wise and the foolish. That is why I am so eager to preach the gospel also to you who are at Rome.

I am not ashamed of the gospel, because it is the power of God for the salvation of everyone who believes: first for the Jew, then for the Gentile. For in the gospel a righteousness from God is revealed, a righteousness that is by faith from first to last, just as it is written: "The righteous will live by faith."

MAN REJECTS GOD, GOD REJECTS MAN

The wrath of God is being revealed from heaven against all the godlessness and wickedness of men who suppress the truth by their wickedness, since what may be known about God is plain to them, because God has made it plain to them. For since the creation of the world God's invisible qualities—his eternal power and divine nature—have been clearly seen, being understood from what has been made, so that men are without excuse.

For although they knew God, they neither glorified him as God nor gave thanks to him, but their thinking became futile and their foolish hearts were darkened. Although they claimed to be wise, they became fools and exchanged the glory of the immortal God for images made to look like mortal man and birds and animals and reptiles.

Therefore God gave them over in the sinful desires of their hearts to sexual impurity for the degrading of their bodies with one another. They exchanged the truth of God for a lie, and worshiped and served created things rather than the Creator— who is forever praised. Amen.

Because of this, God gave them over to shameful lusts. Even their women exchanged natural relations for unnatural ones. In the same way the men also abandoned natural relations with women and were inflamed with lust for one another. Men committed indecent acts with other men, and received in themselves the due penalty for their perversion.

HUMAN THOUGHTS AND ACTIONS

Furthermore, since they did not think it worthwhile to retain the knowledge of God, he gave them over to a depraved mind, to do what ought not to be done. They have become filled with every land of wickedness, evil, greed and depravity. They are full of envy, murder, strife, deceit and malice. They are gossips, slanderers, God-haters, insolent, arrogant and boastful; they invent ways of doing evil; they disobey their parents; they are senseless, faithless, heartless, ruthless. Although they know God's righteous decree that those who do such things deserve death, they not only continue to do these very things but also approve of those who practice them.

JUDGING OTHERS

You, therefore, have no excuse, you who pass judgment on someone else, for at whatever point you judge the other, you are condemning yourself, because you who pass judgment do the same things. Now we know that God's judgment against those who do such things is based on truth. So when you, a mere man, pass judgment on them and yet do the same things, do you think you will escape God's judgment? Or do you show contempt for the riches of his kindness, tolerance and patience, not realizing that God's kindness leads you towards repentance?

GOD'S JUDGMENT

But because of your stubbornness and your unrepentant heart, you are storing up wrath against yourself for the day of God's wrath, when his righteous judgment will be revealed. God "will give to each person according to what he has done." To those who by persistence in doing good seek glory, honor and immortality, he will give eternal life. But for those who are self-seeking and who reject the truth and follow evil, there will be wrath and anger. There will be trouble and distress for every human being who does evil: first for the Jew, then for the Gentile; but glory, honor and peace for everyone who does good: first for the Jew, then for the Gentile. For God does not show favoritism.

GOD JUDGES MEN'S SECRETS

All who sin apart from the law will also perish apart from the law, and all who sin under the law will be judged by the law. For it is not those who hear the law who are righteous in God's sight, but it is those who obey the law who will be declared righteous. (Indeed, when Gentiles, who do not have the law, do by nature things required by the law, they are a law for themselves, even though they do not have the law, since they show that the requirements of the law are written on their hearts, their consciences also bearing witness, and their thoughts now accusing, now even defending them.) This will take place on the day when God will judge men's secrets through Jesus Christ, as my gospel declares.

HYPOCRISY

Now you, if you call yourself a Jew; if you rely on the law and brag about your relationship to God; if you know his will and approve of what is superior because you are instructed by the law; if you are convinced that you are a guide for the blind, a light for those who are in the dark, an instructor of the foolish, a teacher of infants, because you have in the law the embodiment of knowledge and truth—you, then, who teach others, do you not teach yourself? You who preach against stealing, do you steal? You who say that people should not commit adultery, do you commit adultery? You who abhor idols, do you rob temples? You who brag about the law, do you dishonor God by breaking the law? As it is written: "God's name is blasphemed among the Gentiles because of you.". . .

PEOPLE MOVE AWAY FROM GOD

What shall we conclude then? Are we any better? Not at all! We have already made the charge that Jews and Gentiles alike are all under sin. As it is written:

"There is no one righteous, not even one; there is no one who understands, no one who seeks God. All have turned away, they have together become worthless; there is no one who does good, not even one."

"Their throats are open graves; their tongues practice deceit."

"The poison of vipers is on their lips."

"Their mouths are full of cursing and bitterness."

"Their feet are swift to shed blood; ruin and misery mark

their ways, and the way of peace they do not know."

"There is no fear of God before their eyes."

Now we know that whatever the law says, it says to those who are under the law, so that every mouth may be silenced and the whole world held accountable to God. Therefore no one will be declared righteous in his sight by observing the law; rather, through the law we become conscious of sin.

FAITH LEADS TO GOD

But now a righteousness from God, apart from law, has been made known, to which the Law and the Prophets testify. This righteousness from God comes through faith in Jesus Christ to all who believe. There is no difference, for all have sinned and fall short of the glory of God.

"The glorious independence of man in a savage state. This youth . . . was ready at a moment's warning to rove the world . . . and in the absence of artificial wants possessed the great secret of personal freedom."

HUMANS ARE IN CONFLICT WITH NATURE

Washington Irving

For two centuries, Americans have expressed an uncertainty about progress and civilization. While pushing west for land and progress, settlers and those who stayed in the East regretted the lost purity and innocence which resulted. In this viewpoint, Washington Irving (1783–1859) captures these feelings in his observations of the white settlers and the Native American Indians. Washington is a pleasant, yet thought provoking, writer of such works as: "Rip Van Winkle," "The Legend of Sleepy Hollow," and *A History of New York*. This viewpoint suggests that civilized humanity is at odds with the natural environment. As a result, humans seem at odds with themselves.

As you read, consider the following questions:

1. How does Irving describe the "civilized" settler? How does Irving describe the Indian?
2. Irving says that people are not slaves to society. To what are they slaves?
3. What does Irving believe to be the most important goal in life?

Reprinted from chapter 5 of *A Tour on the Prairies*, by Washington Irving (1835).

On the following morning we were on the march by half past seven o'clock, and rode through deep rich bottoms of alluvial soil, overgrown with redundant vegetation and trees of an enormous size. Our route lay parallel to the west bank of the Arkansas, on the borders of which river, near the confluence of the Red Fork, we expected to overtake the main body of rangers. For some miles the country was sprinkled with Creek villages and farm-houses, the inhabitants of which appeared to have adopted, with considerable facility, the rudiments of civilisation, and to have thriven in consequence. Their farms were well stocked, and their houses displayed comfort and abundance.

We met with numbers of them returning from one of those grand games of ball, for which their nation is celebrated. Some were on foot, some on horseback; the latter, occasionally, with gaily dressed females behind them. They are a well-made race, muscular and closely knit, with well-turned thighs and legs. They have a gipsy fondness for brilliant colours and gay decorations, and are bright and fanciful objects when seen at a distance from the prairies. One had a scarlet handkerchief bound round his head, surmounted with a tuft of black feathers like a cock's tail. Another had a white handkerchief, with red feathers; while a third, for want of a plume, had stuck in his turban a brilliant bunch of sumach.

ANGRY WHITE SETTLER

On the verge of the wilderness we paused to enquire our way at a log-house, owned by a white settler or squatter,—a tall, raw-boned old fellow, with red hair, a lank lanthorn visage, and an inveterate habit of winking with one eye, as if every thing he said was of knowing import. He was in a towering passion. One of his horses was missing: he swore it had been stolen in the night by a straggling party of Osages, encamped in a neighbouring swamp. But he would have satisfaction! he would make an example of the villains! He had, accordingly caught down the rifle from the wall, that invariable enforcer of right or wrong upon the frontiers, and, having saddled his steed, was about to sally on a foray into the swamp, while a brother squatter, with rifle in hand, stood ready to accompany him.

We endeavoured to calm the old campaigner of the prairies, by suggesting that his horse might have strayed into the neighbouring woods; but he had the frontier propensity to charge every thing to the fault of the Indians, and nothing could dissuade him from carrying fire and sword into the swamp.

After riding a few miles farther, we lost the trail of the main body of rangers, and became perplexed by a variety of tracks made by the Indians and settlers. . . .

We had not long regained the trail, when, on emerging from a forest, we beheld our raw-boned, hard-winking, hard-riding knight errant of the frontier, [the angry white settler] descending the slope of a hill, followed by his companion in arms. As he drew near to us, the gauntness of his figure, and ruefulness of his aspect, reminded me of the descriptions of the hero of La Mancha; and he was equally bent on affairs of doughty emprize, being about to penetrate the thickets of the perilous swamp, within which the enemy lay ensconced.

NOBLE SAVAGE

While we were holding a parley with him on the slope of the hill, we descried an Osage on horseback, issuing out of a skirt of wood about half a mile off, and leading a horse by a halter. The latter was immediately recognised by our hard-winking friend as the steed of which he was in quest. As the Osage drew near, I was struck with his appearance. He was about nineteen or twenty years of age, but well grown, with the fine Roman countenance common to his tribe; and as he rode, with his blanket wrapped round his loins, his naked bust would have furnished a model for a statuary. He was mounted on a beautiful piebald horse, a mottled white and brown, of the wild breed of the prairies, decorated with a broad collar, from which hung in front a tuft of horsehair dyed of a bright scarlet.

NATURE VERSUS CIVILIZATION

The youth rode slowly up to us with a frank open air, and signified, by means of our interpreter, Beatte, that the horse he was leading had wandered to their camp, and he was now on his way to conduct him back to his owner. I had expected to witness an expression of gratitude on the part of our hard-favoured cavalier, but, to my surprise, the old fellow broke out into a furious passion. He declared that the Indians had carried off his horse in the night, with the intention of bringing him home in the morning, and claiming a reward for finding him; a common practice, as he affirmed, among the Indians. He was, therefore, for tying the young Indian to a tree and giving him a sound lashing; and was quite surprised at the burst of indignation which this novel mode of requiting a service drew from us. Such, however, is too often the administration of law on the frontier; "Lynch's Law," as it is technically termed; in which the plaintiff is apt to be witness, jury, judge, and executioner; and the defendant to be convicted and punished on mere presumption; and in this way, I am convinced, are occasioned many of those heart-burnings and resentments among the Indians which lead to retaliation, and eventuate in Indian wars. When I compared the open, noble countenance, and frank demeanour of the young Osage, with the sinister visage and high-landed conduct of the frontiers-man, I felt little doubt on whose back a lash would be most meritoriously bestowed.

RETURNING TO NATURE

Primitivists believed that man's happiness and well-being decreased in direct proportion to his degree of civilization. They idealized either contemporary cultures nearer to savagery or a previous age in which they believed all men led a simpler and better existence. Precedents for primitivistic and Romantic attraction to wildness exist well back into Western thought, and by the late Middle Ages there were a number of popular traditions about the noble savage. One concerned the mythical Wild Man whom medieval culture represented as having redeeming as well as repulsive characteristics. Captured in his wilderness retreats and brought back to civilization, the Wild Man supposedly made a better knight than ordinary persons. Contact with the wilds was believed to give him exceptional strength, ferocity, and hardiness combined with innocence and an innate nobility.

Roderick Nash, *Wilderness and the American Mind*, 1967.

Being thus obliged to content himself with the recovery of his horse, without the pleasure of flogging the finder into the bargain, the old Lycurgus, or rather Draco, of the frontier, set off growling on his return homewards, followed by his brother squatter.

TRUE FREEDOM

As for the youthful Osage, we were all prepossessed in his favour; the young Count especially, with the sympathies proper to his age and incident to his character, had taken quite a fancy to him—nothing would suit but he must have the young Osage as a companion and squire in his expedition into the wilderness. The youth was easily tempted; and, with the prospect of a safe range over the buffalo prairies, and the promise of a new blanket, he turned his bridle, left the swamp and the encampment of his friends behind him, and set off to follow the Count in his wanderings in quest of the Osage hunters. Such is the glorious independence of man in a savage state. This youth, with his rifle, his blanket, and his horse, was ready, at a moment's warning, to rove the world: he carried all his worldly effects with him; and in the absence of artificial wants possessed the great secret of personal freedom. We of society are slaves, not so much to others as to ourselves; our superfluities are the chains that bind us, impeding every movement of our bodies, and thwarting every impulse of our souls.

"Woman, like much else, is a product elaborated by civilization."

MALE/FEMALE CONFLICTS ARE MOSTLY SOCIAL

Simone de Beauvoir

Simone de Beauvoir (1908–1986) was a French philosopher. While believing that humans have a great deal of freedom over and responsibility for their lives, she also believed that society greatly shapes how we think and act. In the following excerpt, de Beauvoir states that most of the differences between females and males have been caused by the social traditions which each person adopts. De Beauvoir believes that the future might hold very different arrangements for humans. However, she concludes that minor differences between males and females will always exist.

As you read, consider the following questions:

1. How are both sexes victims of the present male and female roles, according to the author?
2. What does de Beauvoir mean when she writes that "the husband wants to find himself in his wife"?
3. How does de Beauvoir visualize a society with complete equality between the genders?

We have seen that in spite of legends no physiological destiny imposes an eternal hostility upon Male and Female as
such; even the famous praying mantis devours her male only for
want of other food and for the good of the species: it is to this,
the species, that all individuals are subordinated, from the top to
the bottom of the scale of animal life. Moreover, humanity is
something more than a mere species: it is a historical development; it is to be defined by the manner in which it deals with
its natural, fixed characteristics, its facticité. Indeed, even with the
most extreme bad faith in the world, it is impossible to demon-
strate the existence of a rivalry between the human male and female of a truly physiological nature. Further, their hostility may
be allocated rather to that intermediate terrain between biology
and psychology: psychoanalysis. . . .

MALE AND FEMALE ROLES

This difference of attitude is manifest on the sexual plane as on
the spiritual plane. The "feminine" woman in making herself
prey tries to reduce man, also, to her carnal passivity; she occu-
pies herself in catching him in her trap, in enchaining him by
means of the desire she arouses in him in submissively making
herself a thing. The emancipated woman, on the contrary, wants
to be active, a taker, and refuses the passivity man means to im-
pose on her. Thus Elise and her emulators deny the values of the
activities of virile type; they put the flesh above the spirit, con-
tingence above liberty, their routine wisdom above creative au-
dacity. But the "modern" woman accepts masculine values: she
prides herself on thinking, taking action, working, creating, on
the same terms as men; instead of seeking to disparage them,
she declares herself their equal.

In so far as she expresses herself in definite action, this claim
is legitimate, and male insolence must then bear the blame. But
in men's defense it must be said that women are wont to con-
fuse the issue. A Mabel Dodge Luhan intended to subjugate D. H.
Lawrence by her feminine charms so as to dominate him spiritually thereafter; many women, in order to show by their suc-
cesses their equivalence to men, try to secure male support by
sexual means; they play on both sides, demanding old-fashioned
respect and modern esteem, banking on their old magic and
their new rights. It is understandable that a man becomes irri-
tated and puts himself on the defensive; but he is also double-
dealing when he requires woman to play the game fairly while
he denies them the indispensable trump cards through distrust
and hostility. Indeed, the struggle cannot be clearly drawn be-

tween them, since woman is opaque in her very being; she stands before man not as a subject but as an object paradoxically endued with subjectivity; she takes herself simultaneously as *self* and as *other*, a contradiction that entails baffling consequences. When she makes weapons at once of her weakness and of her strength, it is not a matter of designing calculation: she seeks salvation spontaneously in the way that has been imposed on her, that of passivity, at the same time when she is actively demanding her sovereignty; and no doubt this procedure is unfair tactics, but it is dictated to her by the ambiguous situation assigned her. Man, however, becomes indignant when he treats her as a free and independent being and then realizes that she is still a trap for him; if he gratifies and satisfies her in her posture as prey, he finds her claims to autonomy irritating; whatever he does, he feels tricked and she feels wronged.

Both Sexes Are Victims

The quarrel will go on as long as men and women fail to recognize each other as peers; that is to say, as long as femininity is perpetuated as such. Which sex is the more eager to maintain it? Woman, who is being emancipated from it, wishes none the less to retain its privileges; and man, in that case, wants her to assume its limitations. "It is easier to accuse one sex than to excuse the other," says [French skeptic Michel de] Montaigne. It is vain to apportion praise and blame. The truth is that if the vicious circle is so hard to break, it is because the two sexes are each the victim at once of the other and of itself. Between two adversaries confronting each other in their pure liberty, an agreement could be easily reached: the more so as the war profits neither. But the complexity of the whole affair derives from the fact that each camp is giving aid and comfort to the enemy; woman is pursuing a dream of submission, man a dream of identification. Want of authenticity does not pay: each blames the other for the unhappiness he or she has incurred in yielding to the temptations of the easy way; what man and woman loathe in each other is the shattering frustration of each one's own bad faith and baseness.

We have seen why men enslaved women in the first place; the devaluation of femininity has been a necessary step in human evolution, but it might have led to collaboration between the two sexes; oppression is to be explained by the tendency of the existent to flee from himself by means of identification with the other, whom he oppresses to that end. In each individual man that tendency exists today; and the vast majority yield to it. The husband wants to find himself in his wife, the lover in his mistress, in the form of a stone image; he is seeking in her the myth of his virility, of his sovereignty, of his immediate reality. "My husband never goes to the movies," says his wife, and the dubious masculine opinion is graved in the marble of eternity. But he is himself the slave of his double: what an effort to build up an image in which he is always in danger! In spite of everything his success in this depends upon the capricious freedom of women: he must constantly try to keep this propitious to him. Man is concerned with the effort to appear male, important, superior; he pretends so as to get pretense in return; he, too, is aggressive, uneasy; he feels hostility for women because he is afraid of them, he is afraid of them because he is afraid of the personage, the image, with which he identifies himself. What time and strength he squanders in liquidating, sublimating, transferring complexes, in talking about women, in seducing them, in fearing them! He would be liberated himself in their liberation. But this is precisely what he dreads. And so he obstinately persists in the mystifications intended to keep woman in her chains. . . .

A Society of Gender Equality

A world where men and women would be equal is easy to visualize, for that precisely is what the Soviet Revolution promised: women raised and trained exactly like men were to work under the same conditions and for the same wages. Erotic liberty was to be recognized by custom, but the sexual act was not to be considered a "service" to be paid for; woman was to be obliged to provide herself with other ways of earning a living; marriage was to be based on a free agreement that the spouses could break at will; maternity was to be voluntary, which meant that contraception and abortion were to be authorized and that, on the other hand, all mothers and their children were to have exactly the same rights, in or out of marriage; pregnancy leaves were to be paid for by the State, which would assume charge of the children, signifying not that they would be taken away from their parents, but that they would not be abandoned to them.

But is it enough to change laws, institutions, customs, public opinion, and the whole social context, for men and women to become truly equal? "Women will always be women," say the skeptics. Other seers prophesy that in casting off their femininity they will not succeed in changing themselves into men and they will become monsters. This would be to admit that the woman of today is a creation of nature; it must be repeated once more that in human society nothing is natural and that woman, like much else, is a product elaborated by civilization. The intervention of others in her destiny is fundamental: if this action took a different direction, it would produce a quite different result. Woman is determined not by her hormones or by mysterious instincts, but by the manner in which her body and her relation to the world are modified through the action of others than herself. The abyss that separates the adolescent boy and girl has been deliberately opened out between them since earliest childhood; later on, woman could not be other than what she *was made*, and that past was bound to shadow her for life. If we appreciate its influence, we see clearly that her destiny is not predetermined for all eternity.

ECONOMIC EQUALITY IS NOT ENOUGH

We must not believe, certainly, that a change in woman's economic condition alone is enough to transform her, though this factor has been and remains the basic factor in her evolution; but until it has brought about the moral, social, cultural, and other consequences that it promises and requires, the new woman cannot appear. At this moment they have been realized nowhere, in Russia no more than in France or the United States; and this explains why the woman of today is torn between the past and the future. She appears most often as a "true woman" disguised as a man, and she feels herself as ill at ease in her flesh as in her masculine garb. She must shed her old skin and cut her own new clothes. This she could do only through a social evolution. No single educator could fashion a *female human being* today who would be the exact homologue of the *male human being*; if she is raised like a boy, the young girl feels she is an oddity and thereby she is given a new kind of sex specification. [French novelist] Stendhal understood this when he said: "The forest must be planted all at once." But if we imagine, on the contrary, a society in which the equality of the sexes would be concretely realized, this equality would find new expression in each individual. . . .

Let us not forget that our lack of imagination always depopulates the future; for us it is only an abstraction; each one of us secretly deplores the absence there of the one who was himself. But the humanity of tomorrow will be living in its flesh and in its conscious liberty; that time will be its present and it will in turn prefer it. New relations of flesh and sentiment of which we have no conception will arise between the sexes; already, indeed, there have appeared between men and women friendships, rivalries, complicities, comradeships—chaste or sensual—which past centuries could not have conceived. To mention one point, nothing could seem to me more debatable than the opinion that dooms the new world to uniformity and hence to boredom. I fail to see that this present world is free from boredom or that liberty ever creates uniformity.

SOME DIFFERENCES WILL ALWAYS EXIST

To begin with, there will always be certain differences between man and woman; her eroticism, and therefore her sexual world, have a special form of their own and therefore cannot fail to engender a sensuality, a sensitivity, of a special nature. This means that her relations to her own body, to that of the male, to the child, will never be identical with those the male bears to his own body, to that of the female, and to the child; those who make much of "equality in difference" could not with good grace refuse to grant me the possible existence of differences in equality. Then again, it is institutions that create uniformity. Young and pretty, the slaves of the harem are always the same in the sultan's embrace; Christianity gave eroticism its savor of sin and legend when it endowed the human female with a soul; if society restores her sovereign individuality to woman, it will not thereby destroy the power of love's embrace to move the heart.

CULTURE SHAPES PERSONALITY

There can be little doubt that in certain cases factors other than the cultural ones are primarily responsible for producing a particular personality configuration. However, it seems that in a majority of cases the cultural factors are dominant. We find that in all societies the personalities of the "average," "normal" individuals who keep the society operating in its accustomed ways can be accounted for in cultural terms. At the same time we find that all societies include atypical individuals whose personalities fall outside the normal range of variation for the society. The causes of such aberrant personalities are still imperfectly understood. They unquestionably derive in part from accidents of early environment and experience. In how far still other, genetically determined factors may be involved we are still unable to say.

Ralph Linton, *The Cultural Background of Personality*, 1945.

It is nonsense to assert that revelry, vice, ecstasy, passion, would become impossible if man and woman were equal in concrete matters; the contradictions that put the flesh in opposition to the spirit, the instant to time, the swoon of immanence to the challenge of transcendence, the absolute of pleasure to the nothingness of forgetting, will never be resolved; in sexuality will always be materialized the tension, the anguish, the joy, the frustration, and the triumph of existence. To emancipate woman is to refuse to confine her to the relations she bears to man, not to deny them to her; let her have her independent existence and she will continue none the less to exist for him *also*: mutually recognizing each other as subject, each will yet remain for the other an *other*. The reciprocity of their relations will not do away with the miracles—desire, possession, love, dream, adventure—worked by the division of human beings into two separate categories; and the words that move us—giving, conquering, uniting—will not lose their meaning. On the contrary, when we abolish the slavery of half of humanity, together with the whole system of hypocrisy that it implies, then the "division" of humanity will reveal its genuine significance and the human couple will find its true form.

"The different languages men and women speak can shake the foundation of our lives."

MALE/FEMALE CONFLICTS ARE MISUNDERSTANDINGS

Deborah Tannen

Deborah Tannen is a scholar in linguistics, or the study of the spoken and written language. Tannen teaches at Georgetown University and has written both scholarly and popular books. She is best known for two widely-read works: *That's Not What I Mean* and *You Just Don't Understand.* These books give insights into why conflicts develop and become prolonged in human relationships. Though she does not help us learn if females and males have different natures, Tannen does help us understand the tension that exists between the sexes.

As you read, consider the following questions:

1. According to Tannen, what are some of the reasons that males and females misunderstand each other?
2. Does Tannen feel that misunderstandings between females and males can be easily resolved?
3. According to Tannen, can males and females change how they communicate?

G ender is a category that will not go away. As Goffman put it, it is "one of the most deeply seated traits of man"(!). We create masculinity and femininity in our ways of behaving, all the while believing we are simply acting "naturally." But our sense of what is natural is different for women and men. And what we regard as naturally male and female is based on asymmetrical alignments.

In Goffman's terms, gender relations are patterned on the parent-child complex. In other words, the ways we enact our genders as we try to be good women and men take on meaning by analogy with parents and children. Goffman points out that men are to women as adults are to children: loving protectors who will hold open doors, offer the first portion of sweets, reach high shelves, and lift heavy loads. But along with the privileges of childhood come liabilities: Children's activities are interruptible, their time and territory expendable. Along with the privilege of being protected comes the loss of rights, and not being respected and treated like a full-fledged person. Being the protector frames someone as competent, capable, and deserving of respect. Being protected frames one as incompetent, incapable, and deserving of indulgence.

ASYMMETRIES IN CONVERSATION: "I ONLY DID IT FOR YOU"

In talking to couples about communication in their relationships, I was surprised by how often men referred to their role as protectors of women in explaining why they spoke as they did. For example, one couple told me of a recent argument. The woman had noticed that her husband was favoring one arm and asked why. He said that his arm hurt. She asked how long it had been hurting him, and he said, "Oh, a few weeks." To his surprise, she reacted with hurt and anger: "Go ahead, treat me like a stranger!"

To her, intimacy meant telling what's on your mind, including what hurts. By not telling her that his arm hurt, her husband was pushing her away, distancing her with his silence. I instinctively understood this woman's point of view. But I did not immediately understand the man's. In explaining his side of the story, he said, "I guess men learn from the beginning to protect women." This puzzled me. I asked what protection had to do with not telling his wife that his arm hurt. "I was protecting her," he explained. "Why should I worry her by telling her about my pain, since it might be nothing and go away anyway?"

Deciding what to tell his wife reflects this man's perceived role as her protector. But it also grows out of and reinforces the alignment by which he is in a superior position. He is stronger than she, and he has power to cause her worry by the information he imparts. This man does not feel, as his wife perceives, that he is trying to curtail their intimacy. Intimacy is simply not at issue for him. In her world, the imparting of personal information is the fundamental material of intimacy, so withholding such information deprives her of the closeness that is her lifeblood. Their different interpretations of the same information simply reflect their different preoccupations. They are tuned to different frequencies.

It may be that this man was also protecting his autonomy, staving off his wife's excessive show of concern. But this was not the reason he offered in explaining his motives. In his explanatory system, his role as protector was primary. The same was true for another husband whose wife complained about a very different type of behavior.

INTENTIONS AND WORDS

The wife, whom I will call Michele, objected to the habit her husband, Gary, had of answering her questions by providing information other than what she had requested. Here are two typical exchanges that she recounted:

MICHELE: What time is the concert?

GARY: You have to be ready by seven-thirty.

MICHELE: How many people are coming to dinner?

GARY: Don't worry. There'll be enough food.

Michele gets frustrated because she feels that by withholding information, Gary is holding tight to the reins of power in the relationship. But he maintains that he is "watching out for her" by getting to the real point of her questions. Both points of view are plausible. The cause of their different interpretations of the same conversation resides in the ambiguity inherent in protecting. He sees his attention to her concerns as protective; she sees that the protective stance frames him as one-up in competence and control.

Another man reported similar conversations with his wife. In this case, however, the roles are reversed: It is the wife, Valerie, who gives what she thinks is the relevant information rather than answering the question asked, and it is the husband, Ned, who objects to her doing so. Here are two examples of their dialogues:

NED: Are you leaving now?

VALERIE: You can take a nap if you want.

NED: Are you just about finished?

VALERIE: Do you want to have supper now?

In defending herself against Ned's complaints, Valerie gives an explanation very different from the one given by the husband in the previous example. She says that she is anticipating Ned's desires and concerns.

DIFFERENT POINTS OF VIEW

This man and woman give different explanations for behaving in the same way; they truly seem to think of themselves as doing the same thing for different reasons. Being the protector is central to him; being helpful is central to her.

If women and men sometimes have (or give) different motivations when they behave in similar ways, there are also situations where their different motivations lead them to behave differently. Each individual works out a unique way of balancing status differences and connection to others. But if we think of these motivations as two ends of a continuum, women and men tend to cluster at opposite ends. Because of these differences in points of view, a man and a woman may perceive the same scene in different ways and misinterpret each other's motives. Understanding the differences can deflect the misinterpretation, and make sense where there seemed to be no sense. . . .

OPENING LINES OF COMMUNICATION

Many experts tell us we are doing things wrong and should change our behavior—which usually sounds easier than it turns out to be. Sensitivity training judges men by women's standards, trying to get them to talk more like women. Assertiveness training judges women by men's standards and tries to get them to talk more like men. No doubt, many people can be helped by learning to be more sensitive or more assertive. But few people are helped by being told they are doing everything all wrong. And there may be little wrong with what people are doing, even if they are winding up in arguments. The problem may be that each partner is operating within a different system, speaking a different genderlect.

An obvious question is, Can genderlect be taught? Can people change their conversational styles? If they want to, yes, they can—to an extent. But those who ask this question rarely want to change their own styles. Usually, what they have in mind is sending their partners for repair: They'd like to get him or her to change. Changing one's own style is far less appealing, because it is not just how you act but who you feel yourself to be. Therefore a more realistic approach is to learn how to interpret each other's messages and explain your own in a way your partner can understand and accept.

UNDERSTANDING DIFFERENCES

Understanding genderlects makes it possible to change—to try speaking differently—when you want to. But even if no one changes, understanding genderlect improves relationships. Once people realize that their partners have different conversational styles, they are inclined to accept differences without blaming themselves, their partners, or their relationships. The biggest mistake is believing there is one right way to listen, to talk, to have a conversation—or a relationship. Nothing hurts more than being told your intentions are bad when you know they are good, or being told you are doing something wrong when you know you're just doing it your way.

Not seeing style differences for what they are, people draw conclusions about personality ("you're illogical," "you're insecure," "you're self-centered") or intentions ("you don't listen," "you put me down"). Understanding style differences for what they are takes the sting out of them. Believing that "you're not interested in me," "you don't care about me as much as I care about you," or "you want to take away my freedom" feels awful. Believing that "you have a different way of showing you're listening" or "showing you care" allows for no-fault negotiation: You can ask for or make adjustments without casting or taking blame.

If you understand gender differences in what I call conversational style, you may not be able to prevent disagreements from arising, but you stand a better chance of preventing them from spiraling out of control. When sincere attempts to communicate end in stalemate, and a beloved partner seems irrational and obstinate, the different languages men and women speak can shake the foundation of our lives. Understanding the other's ways of talking is a giant leap across the communication gap between women and men, and a giant step toward opening lines of communication.

CHAPTER 4

WHAT IS THE FUTURE OF HUMAN NATURE?

CHAPTER PREFACE

Just as writers often look to history to understand the origins of human nature, they also look to the future and wonder what will happen next. In his futuristic novel 1984, George Orwell leads his readers to wonder if certain characteristics of human nature, such as personal freedom, romantic love, and intellectual curiosity, might someday be destroyed by a powerful, manipulative political system. The novel portrays a society in which technology and psychological methods of control are used to attack, and perhaps to destroy, the "human spirit." Orwell gives the reader little, if any, hope that true humanity will survive the forces of "Big Brother."

In contrast, Soviet native Alexander Solzhenitsyn, who endured a powerful and manipulative political system, presents a more hopeful perspective. In his novel One Day in the Life of Ivan Denisovich, Solzhenitsyn shows that human nature can survive and even grow stronger in the face of a totalitarian society. Often the prisoners submit to the dehumanizing forces of the Soviet work camp. Occasionally, however, they are successful in their resistance. Solzhenitsyn depicts the life of a hardened prisoner who not only survives but also finds an inner strength to become stronger in spite of the harsh environment.

Psychologist B.F. Skinner, who denies the existence of human nature, writes in his futuristic novel Walden Two that humans can solve their problems by building a society which will meet every human need. Because there is no human nature, humans are completely shaped by their environment. Skinner reasons that if the environment is poorly designed, people will be in conflict with each other; if the environment is properly planned according to psychological principles, then people will live in harmony and happiness. Skinner is optimistic that, if the principles of behavioristic psychology are properly implemented, humans can build such a utopia.

Skinner's optimism is based on the belief that there is no human nature to limit the future improvements of human living. Social philosopher Lewis Mumford, however, believes that humans do have a nature, but that it is continually evolving. In fact, everything in Mumford's world is evolving; he particularly focuses on how technology, communications, and transportation are breaking down old social and political barriers between humans. A new social environment is developing that is global in scope, and to meet this new environment, humans need to develop a nature that is cooperative and open to new possibilities. Mumford challenges his readers with the idea that humans can adapt themselves to this new environment and develop a new kind of human nature.

The future, whether considered in terms of a few years or a few million years, is inevitable. The following authors give just a few perspectives into understanding what could possibly happen to humanity.

"You are imagining that there is something called human nature which will be outraged by what we do and will turn against us. But we create human nature."

HUMAN NATURE MIGHT BE DESTROYED

George Orwell

The twentieth century began with hopes that humanity was progressing toward greater democracy and justice. However, after the destructiveness of Nazi Germany and the Soviet Union, many writers began to wonder whether individuals would be able to resist totalitarian governments in the future. The selection below is from George Orwell's novel, 1984. Winston is the hero of the novel, who has rebelled against "Big Brother," a future, all-powerful government. In the scene below, Winston is both tortured and brainwashed by O'Brien, who works for the government. One of Winston's acts of rebellion is his love affair with Julia. In the passage, Winston faces the twisted logic of the "Party," or Big Brother. Winston is being forced to give up his faith in human nature, in love, in logic, and in truth.

As you read, consider the following questions:

1. What does O'Brien (the representative of Big Brother) mean when he says, "But we create human nature. Men are infinitely malleable."?
2. Winston has faith in a human spirit to rebel against the Party. To weaken that faith, what does O'Brien show to Winston?

Excerpts adapted from Nineteen Eighty-four, by George Orwell. Copyright 1949 by Harcourt Brace & Company and renewed 1977 by Sonia Brownell Orwell; ©1949 by George Orwell. Reprinted by permission of Harcourt Brace & Company; Mark Hamilton, as Literary Executor of the Estate of the Late Sonia Brownell Orwell; and Martin Secker & Warburg Ltd.

"There are three stages in your reintegration," said O'Brien. "There is learning, there is understanding, and there is acceptance. It is time for you to enter upon the second stage."

As always, Winston was lying flat on his back. But of late his bonds were looser. They still held him to the bed, but he could move his knees a little and could turn his head from side to side and raise his arms from the elbow. The dial, also, had grown to be less of a terror. He could evade its pangs if he was quick-witted enough; it was chiefly when he showed stupidity that O'Brien pulled the lever. Sometimes they got through a whole session without use of the dial. He could not remember how many sessions there had been. The whole process seemed to stretch out over a long, indefinite time—weeks, possibly—and the intervals between the sessions might sometimes have been days, sometimes only an hour or two. . . .

CAN ANYTHING STOP BIG BROTHER?

"You could not create such a world as you have just described. It is a dream. It is impossible."

"Why?"

"It is impossible to found a civilization on fear and hatred and cruelty. It would never endure."

"Why not?"

"It would have no vitality. It would disintegrate. It would commit suicide."

"Nonsense. You are under the impression that hatred is more exhausting than love. Why should it be? And if it were, what difference would that make? Suppose that we choose to wear our-selves out faster. Suppose that we quicken the tempo of human life till men are senile at thirty. Still what difference would it make? Can you not understand that the death of the individual is not death? The Party is immortal."

As usual, the voice had battered Winston into helplessness. Moreover he was in dread that if he persisted in his disagree-ment O'Brien would twist the dial again. And yet he could not keep silent. Feebly, without arguments, with nothing to support him except his inarticulate horror of what O'Brien had said, he returned to the attack.

"I don't know—I don't care. Somehow you will fail. Some-thing will defeat you. Life will defeat you."

IS THERE A HUMAN NATURE?

"We control life, Winston, at all its levels. You are imagining that there is something called human nature which will be outraged

116

by what we do and will turn against us. But we create human nature. Men are infinitely malleable. Or perhaps you have returned to your old idea that the proletarians or the slaves will arise and overthrow us. Put it out of your mind. They are helpless, like the animals. Humanity is the Party. The others are outside—irrelevant."

"I don't care. In the end they will beat you. Sooner or later they will see you for what you are, and then they will tear you to pieces."

"Do you see any evidence that that is happening? Or any reason why it should?"

"No. I believe it. I *know* that you will fail. There is something in the universe—I don't know, some spirit, some principle—that you will never overcome."

"Do you believe in God, Winston?"

"No."

"Then what is it, this principle that will defeat us?"

"I don't know. The spirit of Man."

"And do you consider yourself a man?"

"Yes."

"If you are a man, Winston, you are the last man. Your kind is extinct; we are the inheritors. Do you understand that you are *alone?* You are outside history, you are nonexistent." His manner changed and he said more harshly: "And you consider yourself morally superior to us, with our lies and our cruelty?"

"Yes, I consider myself superior."

O'Brien did not speak. Two other voices were speaking. After a moment Winston recognized one of them as his own. It was a sound track of the conversation he had had with O'Brien, on the night when he had enrolled himself in the Brotherhood. He heard himself promising to lie, to steal, to forge, to murder, to encourage drug taking and prostitution, to disseminate venereal diseases, to throw vitriol in a child's face. O'Brien made a small impatient gesture, as though to say that the demonstration was hardly worth making. Then he turned a switch and the voices stopped.

HUMAN SPIRIT OR HUMAN BODY

"Get up from that bed," he said.

The bonds had loosened themselves. Winston lowered himself to the floor and stood up unsteadily.

"You are the last man," said O'Brien. "You are the guardian of the human spirit. You shall see yourself as you are. Take off your clothes."

Winston undid the bit of string that held his overalls together. The zip fastener had long since been wrenched out of them. He could not remember whether at any time since his arrest he had taken off all his clothes at one time. Beneath the overalls his body was looped with filthy yellowish rags, just recognizable as the remnants of underclothes. As he slid them to the ground he saw that there was a three-sided mirror at the far end of the room. He approached it, then stopped short. An involuntary cry had broken out of him.

CAN HUMANS RESIST?

The question is a philosophical, anthropological and psychological one, and perhaps also a religious one. It is: can human nature be changed in such a way that man will forget his longing for freedom, for dignity, for integrity, for love—that is to say, can man forget that he is human? Or does human nature have a dynamism which will react to the violation of these basic human needs by attempting to change an inhuman society into a human one?

Erich Fromm, "Afterword to 1984," 1961.

"Go on," said O'Brien. "Stand between the wings of the mirror. You shall see the side view as well."

He had stopped because he was frightened. A bowed, gray-colored, skeletonlike thing was coming toward him. Its actual appearance was frightening, and not merely the fact that he knew it to be himself. . . .

WINSTON GIVES UP

He had capitulated; that was agreed. In reality, as he saw now, he had been ready to capitulate long before he had taken the decision. From the moment when he was inside the Ministry of Love—and yes, even during those minutes when he and Julia had stood helpless while the iron voice from the telescreen told them what to do—he had grasped the frivolity, the shallowness of his attempt to set himself up against the power of the Party. He knew now that for seven years the Thought Police had watched him like a beetle under a magnifying glass. There was no physical act, no word spoken aloud, that they had not noticed, no train of thought that they had not been able to infer. Even the speck of whitish dust on the cover of his diary they had carefully replaced. They had played sound tracks to him, shown him photographs. Some of them were photographs of

Julia and himself. Yes, even . . . He could not fight against the Party any longer. Besides, the Party was in the right. It must be so: how could the immortal, collective brain be mistaken? By what external standard could you check its judgments? Sanity was statistical. It was merely a question of learning to think as they thought. Only—!

The pencil felt thick and awkward in his fingers. He began to write down the thoughts that came into his head. He wrote first in large clumsy capitals:

FREEDOM IS SLAVERY.

Then almost without a pause he wrote beneath it:

TWO AND TWO MAKE FIVE.

But then there came a sort of check. His mind, as though shying away from something, seemed unable to concentrate. He knew that he knew what came next, but for the moment he could not recall it. When he did recall it, it was only by consciously reasoning out what it must be; it did not come of its own accord. He wrote:

GOD IS POWER.

He accepted everything. The past was alterable. The past never had been altered. Oceania was at war with Eastasia. Oceania had always been at war with Eastasia. Jones, Aaronson, and Rutherford were guilty of the crimes they were charged with. He had never seen the photograph that disproved their guilt. It had never existed; he had invented it. He remembered remembering contrary things, but those were false memories, products of self-deception. How easy it all was! Only surrender, and everything else followed. It was like swimming against a current that swept you backwards however hard you struggled, and then suddenly deciding to turn round and go with the current instead of opposing it. Nothing had changed except your own attitude; the predestined thing happened in any case. He hardly knew why he had ever rebelled. Everything was easy, except—!

THE HUMAN MIND RESISTS BIG BROTHER

Anything could be true. The so-called laws of nature were nonsense. The law of gravity was nonsense. "If I wished," O'Brien had said, "I could float off this floor like a soap bubble." Winston worked it out. "If he *thinks* he floats off the floor, and if I simultaneously *think* I see him do it, then the thing happens." Suddenly, like a lump of submerged wreckage breaking the surface of water, the thought burst into his mind: "It doesn't really happen. We imagine it. It is hallucination." He pushed the thought under instantly. The fallacy was obvious. It presupposed that somewhere or other, outside oneself, there was a "real" world where "real" things happened. But how could there be such a world? What knowledge have we of anything, save through our own minds? All happenings are in the mind. Whatever happens in all minds, truly happens.

He had no difficulty in disposing of the fallacy, and he was in no danger of succumbing to it. He realized, nevertheless, that it ought never to have occurred to him. The mind should develop a blind spot whenever a dangerous thought presented itself. The process should be automatic, instinctive. *Crimestop*, they called it in Newspeak.

He set to work to exercise himself in crimestop. He presented himself with propositions—"the Party says the earth is flat," "the Party says that ice is heavier than water"—and trained himself in not seeing or not understanding the arguments that contradicted them. It was not easy. It needed great powers of reasoning and improvisation. The arithmetical problems raised, for instance, by such a statement as "two and two make five" were beyond his intellectual grasp. It needed also a sort of athleticism of mind, an ability at one moment to make the most delicate use of logic and at the next to be unconscious of the crudest logical errors. Stupidity was as necessary as intelligence, and as difficult to attain.

Winston Day-Dreams

All the while, with one part of his mind, he wondered how soon they would shoot him. "Everything depends on yourself," O'Brien had said; but he knew that there was no conscious act by which he could bring it nearer. It might be ten minutes hence, or ten years. They might keep him for years in solitary confinement; they might send him to a labor camp; they might release him for a while, as they sometimes did. It was perfectly possible that before he was shot the whole drama of his arrest and interrogation would be enacted all over again. The one certain thing was that death never came at an expected moment. The tradition—the unspoken tradition: somehow you knew it, though you never heard it said—was that they shot you from behind, always in the back of the head, without warning, as you walked down a corridor from cell to cell.

One day—but "one day" was not the right expression; just as probably it was in the middle of the night: once—he fell into a strange, blissful reverie. He was walking down the corridor, waiting for the bullet. He knew that it was coming in another moment. Everything was settled, smoothed out, reconciled. There were no more doubts, no more arguments, no more pain, no more fear. His body was healthy and strong. He walked easily, with a joy of movement and with a feeling of walking in sunlight. He was not any longer in the narrow white corridors of the Ministry of Love; he was in the enormous sunlit passage, a kilometer wide, down which he had seemed to walk in the delirium induced by drugs. He was in the Golden Country, following the foot track across the old rabbit-cropped pasture. He could feel the short springy turf under his feet and the gentle sunshine on his face. At the edge of the field were the elm trees, faintly stirring, and somewhere beyond that was the stream where the dace lay in the green pools under the willows.

HUMAN LOVE RESISTS BIG BROTHER

Suddenly he started up with a shock of horror. The sweat broke out on his backbone. He had heard himself cry aloud:

"Julia! Julia! Julia, my love! Julia!"

For a moment he had had an overwhelming hallucination of her presence. She had seemed to be not merely with him, but inside him. It was as though she had got into the texture of his skin. In that moment he had loved her far more than he had ever done when they were together and free. Also he knew that somewhere or other she was still alive and needed his help.

He lay back on the bed and tried to compose himself. What had he done? How many years had he added to his servitude by that moment of weakness?

In another moment he would hear the tramp of boots outside. They could not let such an outburst go unpunished. They would know now, if they had not known before, that he was breaking the agreement he had made with them. He obeyed the Party, but he still hated the Party.

"His face was all worn-out . . . it was dark and looked like it had been hewed out of stone. . . . You could see his mind was set on one thing— never to give in."

HUMAN NATURE CANNOT BE DESTROYED

Alexander Solzhenitsyn

Some writers have worried that totalitarian governments armed with technology and psychological methods to manipulate people might someday crush the human spirit. In contrast to such theories, Alexander Solzhenitsyn lived through one of the most extreme attempts to control and guide human nature: Soviet Russia and its system of concentration camps (the gulag). The selection below is taken from Solzhenitsyn's novel, *One Day in the Life of Ivan Denisovich*. Briefly, near the end of the novel, an old prisoner, called Y-81, is introduced. Solzhenitsyn uses Y-81 to represent the human spirit, which can remain strong in spite of overwhelming adversity.

As you read, consider the following questions:

1. How does Solzhenitsyn describe the conditions in the work camp?
2. Why are the prisoners fearful of working at the new "Socialist Community Development" project?
3. What qualities can be seen in prisoner Y-81?

From *A Day in the Life of Ivan Denisovich*, by Alexander Solzhenitsyn, translated by Max Hayward and Ronald Hingley. Copyright ©1963 by Henry Holt and Company, Inc. Reprinted by permission of Henry Holt and Company, Inc.

Reveille was sounded, as always, at 5 A.M.—a hammer pounding on a rail outside camp HQ. The ringing noise came faintly on and off through the windowpanes covered with ice more than an inch thick, and died away fast. It was cold and the warder didn't feel like going on banging.

The sound stopped and it was pitch black on the other side of the window, just like in the middle of the night when Shukhov had to get up to go to the latrine, only now three yellow beams fell on the window—from two lights on the perimeter and one inside the camp.

He didn't know why but nobody'd come to open up the barracks. And you couldn't hear the orderlies hoisting the latrine tank on the poles to carry it out.

LIFE IN THE CAMP

Shukhov never slept through reveille but always got up at once. That gave him about an hour and a half to himself before the morning roll call, a time when anyone who knew what was what in the camps could always scrounge a little something on the side. He could sew someone a cover for his mittens out of a piece of old lining. He could bring one of the big gang bosses his dry felt boots while he was still in his bunk, to save him the trouble of hanging around the pile of boots in his bare feet and trying to find his own. Or he could run around to one of the supply rooms where there might be a little job, sweeping or carrying something. Or he could go to the mess hall to pick up bowls from the tables and take piles of them to the dishwashers. That was another way of getting food, but there were always too many other people with the same idea. And the worst thing was that if there was something left in a bowl you started to lick it. You couldn't help it. And Shukhov could still hear the words of his first gang boss, Kuzyomin—an old camp hand who'd already been inside for twelve years in 1943. Once, by a fire in a forest clearing, he'd said to a new batch of men just brought in from the front:

"It's the law of the jungle here, fellows. But even here you can live. The first to go is the guy who licks out bowls, puts his faith in the infirmary, or squeals to the screws."

He was dead right about this—though it didn't always work out that way with the fellows who squealed to the screws. They knew how to look after themselves. They got away with it and it was the other guys who suffered.

Shukhov always got up at reveille, but today he didn't. He'd been feeling lousy since the night before—with aches and pains and the shivers, and he just couldn't manage to keep warm that night. In his sleep he'd felt very sick and then again a little better. All the time he dreaded the morning.

But the morning came, as it always did.

Anyway, how could anyone get warm here, what with the ice piled up on the window and a white cobweb of frost running along the whole barracks where the walls joined the ceiling? And a hell of a barracks it was.

Shukhov stayed in bed. He was lying on the top bunk, with his blanket and overcoat over his head and both his feet tucked in the sleeve of his jacket. He couldn't see anything, but he could tell by the sounds what was going on in the barracks and in his own part of it. He could hear the orderlies tramping down the corridor with one of the twenty-gallon latrine tanks. This was supposed to be light work for people on the sick list—but it was no joke carrying the thing out without spilling it! Then someone from Gang 75 dumped a pile of felt boots from the drying room on the floor. And now someone from his gang did the same (it was also their turn to use the drying room today). The gang boss and his assistant quickly put on their boots, and their bunk creaked. The assistant gang boss would now go and get the bread rations. And then the boss would take off for the Production Planning Section (PPS) at HQ.

THE STUDY OF HUMAN NATURE IS NECESSARY

Unless we have a reasonably clear idea of man as he *is*, as he *might be*, and as he *should be*, we cannot distinguish between those evils that can be modified or eliminated and those evils that are intrinsic to the human condition and must be borne. If we cannot make this distinction, and if we have no settled ideal of man toward which to work, we subject ourselves to the deepening clash of partial and passionate views, generating heat rather than light, obscuring fundamental issues, and encouraging the very "dehumanization" of man that everybody claims to be seeking to avoid.

Philip H. Rhinelander, *Is Man Incomprehensible to Man?* 1973.

But, Shukhov remembered, this wasn't just the same old daily visit to the PPS clerks. Today was the big day for them. They'd heard a lot of talk of switching their gang—104—from putting up workshops to a new job, building a new "Socialist Community Development." But so far it was nothing more than bare fields covered with snowdrifts, and before anything could be done there, holes had to be dug, posts put in, and barbed wire put up—by the prisoners for the prisoners, so they couldn't get out. And then they could start building.

You could bet your life that for a month there'd be no place where you could get warm—not even a hole in the ground. And you couldn't make a fire—what could you use for fuel? So your only hope was to work like hell.

The gang boss was worried and was going to try to fix things, try to palm the job off on some other gang, one that was a little slower on the uptake. Of course you couldn't go empty-handed. It would take a pound of fatback for the chief clerk. Or even two.

Maybe Shukhov would try to get himself on the sick list so he could have a day off. There was no harm in trying. His whole body was one big ache. Then he wondered—which warder was on duty today?

He remembered that it was Big Ivan, a tall, scrawny sergeant with black eyes. The first time you saw him he scared the pants off you, but when you got to know him he was the easiest of all the duty warders—wouldn't put you in the can [jail] or drag you off to the disciplinary officer. So Shukhov could stay put till it was time for Barracks 9 to go to the mess hall. . . .

SHUKHOV IS CAUGHT

Shukhov stayed where he was, on the hard-packed sawdust of his mattress. If only it was one thing or another—either a high fever or an end to the pain. But this way he didn't know where he was.

While the Baptist was whispering his prayers, the Captain came back from the latrine and said to no one in particular, but sort of gloating:

"Brace yourselves, men! It's at least twenty below."

Shukhov made up his mind to go to the infirmary.

And then some strong hand stripped his jacket and blanket off him. Shukhov jerked his quilted overcoat off his face and raised himself up a bit. Below him, his head level with the top of the bunk, stood the Thin Tartar.

So this bastard had come on duty and sneaked up on them.

"S-854!" the Tartar read from the white patch on the back of the black coat. "Three days in the can with work as usual."

The minute they heard his funny muffled voice everyone in the entire barracks—which was pretty dark (not all the lights were on) and where two hundred men slept in fifty bug-ridden bunks—came to life all of a sudden. Those who hadn't yet gotten up began to dress in a hurry.

"But what for, Comrade Warder?" Shukhov asked, and he made his voice sound more pitiful than he really felt.

The can was only half as bad if you were given normal work. You got hot food and there was no time to brood. Not being let out to work—that was real punishment.

HUMANS NEED SPIRITUAL GUIDANCE

It is important to make it abundantly clear at this point that the crucial problem is the spiritual problem, and we here mean by spiritual that area which is the object of attention in philosophy and theology as against that area in which the object of attention is mechanical contrivance. The fact that our life is so gravely threatened in the brightest day of technical achievement is not a criticism of the engineers *qua* engineers, but it is a criticism of all of us as *men*. The paradox of failure at the moment of success is by no means a condemnation of technical progress, for such progress is morally neutral. It gives the surgeon's knife, and it gives the gangster's weapon. Our predicament is a commentary, not on instruments and instrument makers, but on the human inability to employ both scientific knowledge and technical achievement to bring about the good life and the good society. Man is an animal who is peculiarly in need of something to buttress and to guide his spiritual life. Without this, the very capacities that make him a little lower than the angels lead to his destruction. The beasts do not need a philosophy or a religion, but man does.

D. Elton Trueblood, *The Predicament of Modern Man*, 1944.

"Why weren't you up yet? Let's go to the Commandant's office," the Tartar drawled—he and Shukhov and everyone else knew what he was getting the can for.

There was a blank look on the Tartar's hairless, crumpled face. He turned around and looked for somebody else to pick on, but everyone—whether in the dark or under a light, whether on a bottom bunk or a top one—was shoving his legs into the black, padded trousers with numbers on the left knee. Or they were already dressed and were wrapping themselves up and hurrying for the door to wait outside till the Tartar left. . . .

SHUKHOV NOTICES THE OLD MAN

Shukhov was finishing his gruel and hadn't really bothered to take in who was sitting around him. He didn't have to because he'd eaten his own good share of gruel and wasn't on the lookout for anybody else's.

But all the same he couldn't help seeing a tall old man, Y-81, sit down on the other side of the table when somebody got up. Shukhov knew he was from Gang 64, and in the line at the package room he'd heard it was 64 that had gone to the Socialist Community Development today in place of 104. They'd been there all day out in the cold putting up barbed wire to make a compound for themselves.

Shukhov had been told that this old man'd been in camps and prisons more years than you could count and had never come under any amnesty. When one ten-year stretch was over they slapped on another. Shukhov took a good look at him close up. In the camp you could pick him out among all the men with their bent backs because he was straight as a ramrod. When he sat at the table it looked like he was sitting on something to raise himself up higher. There hadn't been anything to shave off his head for a long time—he'd lost all his hair because of the good life. His eyes didn't shift around the mess hall all the time to see what was going on, and he was staring over Shukhov's head and looking at something nobody else could see. He ate his thin gruel with a worn old wooden spoon, and he took his time. He didn't bend down low over the bowl like all the others did, but brought the spoon up to his mouth. He didn't have a single tooth either top or bottom—he chewed the bread with his hard gums like they were teeth. His face was all worn-out but not like a "goner's"—it was dark and looked like it had been hewed out of stone. And you could tell from his big rough hands with the dirt worked in them he hadn't spent many of his long years doing any of the soft jobs. You could see his mind was set on one thing—never to give in. He didn't put his eight ounces [of bread] in all the filth on the table like everybody else but laid it on a clean little piece of rag that'd been washed over and over again.

> "For who can set bounds to man's emergence or to his power of surpassing his provisional achievements?"

THE FUTURE REQUIRES A NEW KIND OF HUMAN NATURE

Lewis Mumford

Lewis Mumford is a social theorist, who has written widely about history and society. For example, he has studied the role cities have had on human life throughout history. He is also interested in the role technology has played in changing our lives and how we look at ourselves. In *The Transformations of Man*, Mumford looks into the future and challenges humanity to prepare itself for a "One World" civilization. While expressing concern about the failures of humanity, Mumford does not have a negative view of humanity's future. He is optimistic that just as humans have evolved in the past, further evolution is possible. His concern is that humans need to start preparing for the future by developing a new kind of human nature.

As you read, consider the following questions:

1. How does Mumford view the future of humanity?
2. When Mumford writes that humanity has always been involved in "self fabrication," what does he mean?
3. What does Mumford mean when he writes, "One World man will seem ideologically and culturally naked"?

The kind of person called for by the present situation is one capable of breaking through the boundaries of culture and history, which have so far limited human growth. A person not indelibly marked by the tattooings of his tribe or restricted by the taboos of his totem: not sewed up for life in the stiff clothes of his caste and calling or encased in vocational armor he cannot remove even when it endangers his life. A person not kept by his religious dietary restrictions from sharing spiritual food that other men have found nourishing; and finally, not prevented by his ideological spectacles from ever getting more than a glimpse of the world as it shows itself to men with other ideological spectacles, or as it discloses itself to those who may, with increasing frequency, be able without glasses to achieve normal vision.

The immediate object of world culture is to break through the premature closures, the corrosive conflicts, and the cyclical frustrations of history. This breakthrough would enable modern man to take advantage of the peculiar circumstances today that favor a universalism that earlier periods could only dream about. But the ultimate purpose of One World culture is to widen the human prospect and open up new domains—on earth, not in interstellar space—for human development. . . .

ALL CULTURES SHOULD BE RESPECTED

The resources for this human transformation have been available for only little more than a century; and many of the technical instruments and corporate agencies have still to be shaped. But for the first time in history, man now begins to know his planet as a whole and to respond to all the peoples who inhabit it: that is, he begins to see his own multiple image in a common mirror, or rather, in a moving picture that traverses backward and forward the dimension of time. Since the exploration of the earth was undertaken by Western man before he was spiritually prepared for it, the peoples and regions that were drawn together by trade, colonization, and conquest lost many of the most precious attributes of their cultures and their personalities. The New World expansion barbarized the conquerors instead of civilizing the conquered. By the same token, Western man impoverished his own future development, too, for the heritage he mangled and often extirpated was also his own, as a member of the human race. In his land hunger, in his greed for gold and silver, for coal and iron and oil, Western man overlooked far greater riches.

Though our dawning sense of interdependence and unity comes too belatedly to repair all the damage that has been done, we see that even the residue of past cultures still holds more values than any single nation has yet created or expressed. By his very consciousness of history, modern man may free himself at last from unconscious compulsions, derived from situations he has outlived, which continue to push him off the highway of development into rubbish-filled blind alleys. Yet if he achieves a fresh understanding of the potentialities he has buried through his own failure to know himself, he may repair his shattered confidence in his future and throw open new vistas. . . .

COMPLEXITY OF THE HUMAN SOUL

This exploration of nature has naturally opened up man's inner history, too. Within the individual soul man finds in symbolic form a whole universe that seems to contain the scattered debris of past cultures and the germinal nodes of future ones. Here, within himself, he finds primitive urges and civilized constraints, tribal fixations and axial liberations, animal lethargies and angelic flights. Through the agency of culture, if not through any more direct impress upon the psyche, all of man's past selves remain disconcertingly alive. Just as man's interpretation of the so-called physical world has now become multidimensional, spanning the whole distance from interstellar to intra-atomic space, and including an exact knowledge of phenomena, like ultraviolet rays, which are outside his sensory experience, so with the inner world of man: it ranges from the depths of the unconscious to the highest levels of conscious ideation, disciplined feeling, and purposeful action. . . .

Now the persistence of old biological or historic residues, whether active or inert, does not mean, as many still falsely suppose, that they have a preappointed or fated outcome. If certain aspects of man's nature are relatively fixed, since they are structured in his organs, they function like the warp in the loom: not merely is there considerable play in the fixed threads themselves, but the shuttle that weaves the fabric lies in man's hands, and by his conscious efforts, introducing new colors and figures, he modifies even the over-all design. Every culture attaches different estimates to man's nature and history; and in its creative moments, it adds new values that enlarge the human personality and give it new destinations. Though man's release from nature's conditions or his own past selves can never be complete, the effort to achieve it is what gives individuality to every historic form: this indeed is what keeps even the most repetitive movements of history from being entirely meaningless. The making of the future is an essential part of man's self-revelation.

The problem for man today is to use his widened consciousness of natural processes and of his own historic nature to promote his own further growth. Such knowledge must now be turned to fuller uses, in the projection of a fresh plan of life and a new image of the self, which shall be capable of rising above man's present limitations and disabilities. This effort, as we have seen, is an old one; for even before man achieved any degree of self-consciousness, he was actively engaged in self-fabrication. If "Be yourself" is nature's first injunction to man, "Transform yourself" was her second—even as "Transcend yourself" seems, at least up to now, to be her final imperative. What will distinguish the present effort to create world culture, if once it takes form, is the richness and variety of the resources that are now open, and the multitude of people now sufficiently released from the struggle for existence to play a part in this new drama. . . .

CHANGING IMAGES OF HUMANITY

Every transformation of man, except that perhaps which produced neolithic culture, has rested on a new metaphysical and ideological base; or rather, upon deeper stirrings and intuitions whose rationalized expression takes the form of a new picture of the cosmos and the nature of man. Even neolithic man may have been no exception; for who can say what images of fertility, what intuitions of the relation of seed and soil, phallus and womb, may not have been the prelude to that order? Our hope of creating one world within and without, accessible in all its reaches to all men, prompting a life more copious, vehement, and bold than any that has appeared before, rests upon a corresponding ideological change. To achieve unity between men, we must cultivate unity within ourselves: to enact that unity, we must have a vision of it before our eyes. . . .

To reach full human stature, at the present stage of development, each of us must be ready, as opportunity offers, to assimilate the contributions of other cultures; and to develop, for the sake of wholeness, those parts of his personality that are weakest. Not least, he must renounce perfection in any single field for the sake of balance and continued growth. He who belongs exclusively to a single nation, a single party, a single religion, or a single vocation without any touch or admixture from the world beyond is not yet a full man, still less can he take part in this transformation. This is a fundamental lesson of human growth, always true—but now imperatively true. In its critical moment of integration, Christianity took in Persian and Egyptian myths, Greek philosophy, and Roman organization, just as

131

Mohammedanism took in the lessons of Moses and Zoroaster and Jesus. So One World man will embrace an even wider circle; and the whole person so created will cast aside the series of masks, some weakly benign, some monstrous, that so long concealed the living features of man.

THE NEW HUMANITY

In his very completeness, One World man will seem ideologically and culturally naked, almost unidentifiable. He will be like the Jain saints of old, "clothed in space," his nakedness a sign that he does not belong exclusively to any nation, group, trade, sect, school, or community. He who has reached the level of world culture will be at home in any part of that culture: in its inner world no less than its outer world. Everything that he does or feels or makes will bear the imprint of the larger self he has made his own. Each person, no matter how poorly endowed or how humble, is eligible to take part in this effort, and indeed is indispensable; yet no matter how great any individual's talents may be, the results will always be incomplete; for the equilibrium we seek is a dynamic one and the balance we promote is not an end in itself but a means to further growth. "It is provided in the essence of things," as Walt Whitman said, "that from any fruition of success, no matter what, shall come forth something to make a greater struggle necessary."

THE FUTURE EVOLUTION OF HUMANITY

Man's evolution is based on the fact that he has lost his original home—nature—and that he can never return to it, can never become an animal again. There is only one way he can take: to emerge fully from his natural home, to find a new home—one which he creates, by making the world a human one and by becoming truly human himself. . . .

The problem of man's existence, then, is unique in the whole of nature; he has fallen out of nature, as it were, and is still in it; he is partly divine, partly animal; partly infinite, partly finite. The necessity to find ever-new solutions for the contradictions in his existence, to find ever-higher forms of unity with nature, his fellow men and himself, is the source of all psychic forces which motivate man, of all his passions, affects and anxieties.

Erich Fromm, *The Sane Society*, 1955.

So we stand on the brink of a new age: the age of an open world and of a self capable of playing its part in that larger sphere. An age of renewal, when work and leisure and learning and love will unite to produce a fresh form for every stage of life, and a higher trajectory for life as a whole. Archaic man, civilized man, axial man, mechanized man, achieved only a partial development of human potentialities; and though much of their work is still viable and useful as a basis for man's further development, no mere quarrying of stones from their now-dilapidated structures will provide material for building the fabric of world culture. No less important than the past forces that drive men on are the new forms, dimly emerging in man's unconscious, that begin to beckon him and hold before him the promise of creativity: a life that will not be at the mercy of chance or fettered to irrelevant necessities. He will begin to shape his whole existence in the forms of love as he once only shaped the shadowy figments of his imagination—though, under the compulsions of his post-historic nihilism he now hardly dares thus to shape even purely aesthetic objects. But soon perhaps the dismembered bones will again knit together, clothed in flesh.

In carrying man's self-transformation to this further stage, world culture may bring about a fresh release of spiritual energy that will unveil new potentialities, no more visible in the human self today than radium was in the physical world a century ago, though always present. Even on its lowest terms, world culture will weld the nations and tribes together in a more meaningful network of relations and purposes. But unified man himself is no terminal point. For who can set bounds to man's emergence or to his power of surpassing his provisional achievements? So far we have found no limits to the imagination, nor yet to the sources on which it may draw. Every goal man reaches provides a new starting point, and the sum of all man's days is just a beginning.

| "Men are made good or bad and wise or foolish by the environment in which they grow."

HUMANS CAN BUILD UTOPIA

B.F. Skinner

Behaviorist psychology is one of many schools of thought in the discipline of psychology. B.F. Skinner (1903–1990) led behaviorism for many years by doing research and by writing many popular books about behaviorism. The following selection is taken from his novel, *Walden Two*. This novel tells the story of several visitors coming to an experimental community called Walden Two. The imaginary community was established by Frazier (who represents the actual beliefs of Skinner) and others to show that behaviorist theories are correct. Life at Walden Two is carefully planned so that everyone "feels" free and happy. The following viewpoint gives a few of the discussions between Frazier and the visitors.

As you read, consider the following questions:

1. According to Frazier, are humans naturally good or bad?
2. Why does Frazier argue in *Walden Two* that social planning is necessary?
3. Castle, who is against Frazier in the novel, wants to protect human freedom. Why does Frazier talk about giving people a "feeling of freedom" and "sense of freedom"?

We returned to the dining rooms by way of a kitchen door. Frazier came up as we were being served, and pointed to the large central table in one of the modern rooms, to which he had just moved his tray.

"Well," he said, as we began to eat, "there isn't much left to show you. We've shot our bolt. I'm curious to know whether you've been properly impressed?"

"'Impressed' is scarcely the word," I said. "It's the most soul-shaking experience of my life."

"A very interesting experiment, there's no doubt about that," said Castle. "Utopia come to life, apparently."

UTOPIA CAN BE REAL

"Utopia, indeed," said Frazier. "And do you know what single fact I find most incredible?" He looked eagerly from one of us to the other, particularly at Rodge, and I began to wonder whether he was not satisfied with two converts out of six.

"The fact that it's been a success, I should imagine," I said.

"What's incredible about that? How could it possibly have failed? No, I'm referring to a detail which distinguishes Walden Two from all the imaginary Utopias ever dreamed of. And a very simple thing, too." He continued to look at us, but we were completely at sea.

"Why, the fact that it exists right here and now!" he announced at last. "In the very midst of modern civilization!" He watched for the effect upon us, but it could not have been very marked.

"The Utopias *have* tended to be a bit out of things," said Castle at last, a little doubtfully, but beginning to get the point.

"Out of things! I should say! Why, 'Utopia' is Greek for 'nowhere,' and Butler spelled 'nowhere' backwards! Bacon chose a lost Atlantis, and Shangri-La is cut off by the highest mountains in the world. Bellamy and Morris felt it necessary to get away by a century or two in the dimension of time. Out of things, indeed! It's the first rule of the Utopian romance: 'Get away from life as we know it, either in space or time, or no one will believe you!'

"The one fact that I would cry from every housetop is this: the Good Life is waiting for us—here and now!" he continued. I almost fancied I heard a Salvation Army drum throbbing in the distance. "It doesn't depend on a change in government or on the machinations of world politics. It doesn't wait upon an improvement in human nature. At this very moment we have the necessary techniques, both material and psychological, to create a full and satisfying life for everyone."

"The trick is to put those techniques into effect," said Castle. "You still have to solve the practical problems of government and politics."

GOVERNMENTS CANNOT SOLVE THE PROBLEMS

"Government and politics! It's not a problem of government and politics at all. That's the first plank in the Walden Two platform. You can't make progress toward the Good Life by political action! Not under *any* current form of government! You must operate upon another level entirely. What you need is a sort of Nonpolitical Action Committee: keep out of politics and away from government except for practical and temporary purposes. It's not the place for men of good will or vision.

"As we use the term these days, government means power—mainly the power to compel obedience," Frazier went on. "The techniques of government are what you would expect—they use force or the threat of force. But that's incompatible with permanent happiness—we know enough about human nature to be sure of that. You can't force a man to be happy. He isn't even likely to be happy if he's *forced* to follow a supposedly happy pattern. He must be led into it in a different way if it's to be satisfying.". . .

"It sounds a little like the old program of anarchy," said Castle.

"By no means. I'm not arguing for no government at all, but only for none of the existing forms. We want a government based upon a science of human behavior. Nothing short of that will produce a permanent social structure. For the first time in history we're ready for it, because we can now deal with human behavior in accordance with simple scientific principles. The trouble with the program of anarchy was that it placed too much faith in human nature. It was an offshoot of the philosophy of perfectionism."

"But you yourself seem to have unbounded faith in human nature," I said.

"I have none at all," said Frazier bluntly, "if you mean that men are naturally good or naturally prepared to get along with each other. We have no truck with philosophies of innate goodness—or evil, either, for that matter. But we do have faith in our power to change human behavior. We can make men adequate for group living—to the satisfaction of everybody. That was our faith, but it's now a fact.". . .

SOCIAL PLANNING IS NECESSARY

"I've admitted neither power nor despotism. But you're quite right in saying that I've exerted an influence and in one sense will continue to exert it forever. I believe you called me a *primum mobile*—not quite correctly, as I found upon looking the term up last night. But I did plan Walden Two—not as an architect plans a building, but as a scientist plans a long-term experiment, uncertain of the conditions he will meet but knowing how he will deal with them when they arise. In a sense, Walden Two is predetermined, but not as the behavior of a beehive is determined. Intelligence, no matter how much it may be shaped and extended by our educational system, will still function as intelligence. It will be used to puzzle out solutions to problems to which a beehive would quickly succumb. What the plan does is to keep intelligence on the right track, for the good of society rather than of the intelligent individual—or for the eventual rather than the immediate good of the individual. It does this by making sure that the individual will not forget his personal stake in the welfare of society."

The Environment Is Responsible

The real issue is the effectiveness of techniques of control. We shall not solve the problems of alcoholism and juvenile delinquency by increasing a sense of responsibility. It is the environment which is "responsible" for the objectional behavior, and it is the environment, not some attribute of the individual, which must be changed. We recognize this when we talk about the punitive contingencies in the natural environment. Running head-on into a wall is punished by a blow to the skull, but we do not hold a man responsible for not running into walls nor do we say that nature holds him responsible. Nature simply punishes him when he runs into a wall. When we make the world less punishing or teach people how to avoid natural punishments, as by giving them rules to follow, we are not destroying responsibility or threatening any other occult quality. We are simply making the world safer.

B.F. Skinner, *Beyond Freedom and Dignity*, 1971.

"But you are forestalling many possibly useful acts of intelligence which aren't encompassed by your plan. You have ruled out points of view which may be more productive. You are implying that T.E. Frazier, looking at the world from the middle of the twentieth century, understands the best course for mankind forever."

"Yes, I suppose I do."

"But that's absurd!"

"Not at all. I don't say I foresee the course man will take a hundred years hence, let alone forever, but I know which he should take now."

"How can you be sure of it? It's certainly not a question you have answered experimentally."

"I think we're in the course of answering it," said Frazier. "But that's beside the point. There's no alternative. We must take that course."

"But that's fantastic. You who are taking it are in a small minority."

Frazier sat up.

"And the majority are in a big quandary," he said. "They're not on the road at all, or they're scrambling back toward their starting point, or sidling from one side of the road to the other like so many crabs. What do you think two world wars have been about? Something as simple as boundaries or trade? Nonsense. The world is trying to adjust to a new conception of man in relation to men."

"Perhaps it's merely trying to adjust to despots whose ideas are incompatible with the real nature of man."

"Mr. Castle," said Frazier very earnestly, "let me ask you a question. I warn you, it will be the most terrifying question of your life. *What would you do if you found yourself in possession of an effective science of behavior?* Suppose you suddenly found it possible to control the behavior of men as you wished. What would you do?"

"That's an assumption?"

"Take it as one if you like. I take it as fact. And apparently you accept it as a fact too. I can hardly be as despotic as you claim unless I hold the key to an extensive practical control."

"What would I do?" said Castle thoughtfully. "I think I would dump your science of behavior in the ocean."

"And deny men all the help you could otherwise give them?"

"And give them the freedom they would otherwise lose forever!"

"How could you give them freedom?"

"By refusing to control them!"

"But you would only be leaving the control in other hands."

"Whose?"

"The charlatan, the demagogue, the salesman, the ward heeler, the bully, the cheat, the educator, the priest—all who are now in possession of the techniques of behavioral engineering."

"A pretty good share of the control would remain in the hands of the individual himself."

"That's an assumption, too, and it's your only hope. It's your only possible chance to avoid the implications of a science of behavior. If man is free, then a technology of behavior is impossible. But I'm asking you to consider the other case."

"Then my answer is that your assumption is contrary to fact and any further consideration idle."

"And your accusations—?"

"—were in terms of intention, not of possible achievement."

Frazier sighed dramatically.

"It's a little late to be proving that a behavioral technology is well advanced. How can you deny it? Many of its methods and techniques are really as old as the hills. Look at their frightful misuse in the hands of the Nazis! And what about the techniques of the psychological clinic? What about education? Or religion? Or practical politics? Or advertising and salesmanship? Bring them all together and you have a sort of rule-of-thumb technology of vast power. No, Mr. Castle, the science is there for the asking. But its techniques and methods are in the wrong hands— they are used for personal aggrandizement in a competitive world or, in the case of the psychologist and educator, for futilely corrective purposes. My question is, have you the courage to take up and wield the science of behavior for the good of mankind? You answer that you would dump it in the ocean!". . .

THE FEELING OF FREEDOM

"The question is: Can men live in freedom and peace? And the answer is: Yes, if we can build a social structure which will satisfy the needs of everyone and in which everyone will want to observe the supporting code. But so far this has been achieved only in Walden Two. Your ruthless accusations to the contrary, Mr. Castle, this is the freest place on earth. And it is free precisely because we make no use of force or the threat of force. Every bit of our research, from the nursery through the psychological management of our adult membership, is directed toward that end—to exploit every alternative to forcible control. By skillful planning, by a wise choice of techniques we *increase* the feeling of freedom.

"It's not planning which infringes upon freedom, but planning which uses force. A sense of freedom was practically unknown in the planned society of Nazi Germany, because the planners made a fantastic use of force and the threat of force.

"No, Mr. Castle, when a science of behavior has once been achieved, there's no alternative to a planned society. We can't leave mankind to an accidental or biased control. But by using the principle of positive reinforcement—carefully avoiding force or the threat of force—we can preserve a personal sense of freedom.". . .

The Environment Creates Humanity

"But the triumph of democracy doesn't mean it's the best government. It was merely the better in a contest with a conspicuously bad one [Fascism of World War II]. Let's not stop with democracy. It isn't, and can't be, the best form of government, because it's based on a scientifically invalid conception of man. It fails to take account of the fact that in the long run *man is determined by the state*. A *laissez-faire* philosophy which trusts to the inherent goodness and wisdom of the common man is incompatible with the observed fact that men are made good or bad and wise or foolish by the environment in which they grow."

"But which comes first," I asked, "the hen or the egg? Men build society and society builds men. Where do we start?"

"It isn't a question of starting. The start has been made. It's a question of what's to be done from now on."

"Then it's to be revolution, is that it?" said Castle. "If democracy can't change itself into something better—"

"Revolution? You're not a very rewarding pupil, Mr. Castle. The change won't come about through power politics at all. It will take place at another level altogether."

"What level?"

Frazier waved his hand toward the window, through which we could see the drenched landscape of Walden Two.

FOR FURTHER DISCUSSION

CHAPTER 1

1. Jean-Paul Sartre writes that there is no human nature. Mortimer Adler affirms that human nature does exist. Imagine a conversation in which they discuss this issue. On what points would they agree? Where would they disagree?

2. Erich Fromm views humans as greatly influenced by social forces. Edward Wilson believes that humans are greatly influenced by biological forces (genetics). How would they respond to George Morgan's claim that humans are free and able to rise above social and biological pressures?

3. Sartre strongly states that humans are free to shape their own existence. What would he say about Wilson's stance that humans are controlled by their biology?

CHAPTER 2

1. Riane Eisler assumes that humans were once cooperative with each other. She suggests that something happened in human social evolution to make people aggressive and competitive with each other. How would Eisler respond to Hobbes' view that each individual is naturally and eternally aggressive toward other humans?

2. Is there a way to harmonize Eisler's ideas with Darwin's understanding of human evolution?

3. Jean-Jacques Rousseau's ideas suggest that humans have evolved, but that evolution has not been positive. In what ways does he agree with the ideas of Darwin and Eisler?

4. How would Rousseau respond to the Genesis account of human creation and human sin?

CHAPTER 3

1. Imagine a conversation between Blaise Pascal and Simone de Beauvoir. He focuses on the inner conflicts in our lives and she focuses on the social conflicts in our lives. In what ways could the two authors agree with each other? What issues would constantly divide them?

2. Deborah Tannen writes that misunderstandings can be very harmful in our lives. Can her ideas complement the ideas of Washington Irving?

3. Is there a way to harmonize the ideas expressed by the Apostle Paul and the ideas of de Beauvoir? Paul writes that human problems are rooted in humanity's tensions with God. Could

such tensions with God result in social consequences? Is there a way to harmonize the ideas of Paul with the ideas of Barfield? If males and females are born with certain tendencies, could it be that humans are born with certain spiritual tendencies?

CHAPTER 4

1. George Orwell's novel suggests that "Big Brother" might destroy the human spirit within the main character, Winston. Alexander Solzhenitsyn's novel suggests that the Soviet system cannot destroy the human spirit in the prisoner labeled Y-81. Is there a human spirit which all humans share? Can it be defined? Can it be destroyed, harmed, or nurtured?

2. Lewis Mumford writes that humans must take control of their own evolution. If we are products of the evolutionary processes, how can we step outside those processes, evaluate those processes, and change those processes? B.F. Skinner presents a similar situation in his novel, *Walden Two*. How can psychologists (who are products of social conditioning) objectively study their social environment? Can products of society (the psychologists) evaluate society and correctly plan ways to improve that society?

3. How would Skinner explain the behavior of Solzhenitsyn's prisoner, Y-81? How would Mumford explain such behavior?

BIBLIOGRAPHY OF BOOKS

Reading the full texts from which the previous viewpoints were taken is highly recommended. In addition to those texts, the following works are recommended for further study.

Donald C. Abel — *Theories of Human Nature: Classical and Contemporary Readings*. New York: McGraw-Hill, 1992. This is a collection of fifteen writers who represent various viewpoints on human nature.

Mortimer J. Adler — *The Great Ideas: A Syntopicon of Great Books of the Western World*, in *The Great Books of the Western World*, edited by Robert Maynard Hutchins. Chicago: Encyclopaedia Britannica, 1952. In volume II of the Syntopicon, the editors give a brief discussion of how the generic term "man" has been used throughout Western thought. An index is also given to guide the reader to passages dealing with human nature throughout the Great Books series.

Mortimer J. Adler — *Ten Philosophical Mistakes*. New York: Collier/Macmillan: 1985. Adler's discussion of human nature in chapter eight is very helpful in understanding current assumptions about human nature in philosophy and psychology. He shows that humans have common "potentialities"—that is, a human nature. However, those potentialities are developed in unique ways by each culture and each individual.

Gordon W. Allport — *Becoming: Basic Considerations for a Psychology of Personality*. New Haven: Yale University Press, 1955. This is an example of how a humanistic psychologist understands human nature. Allport's ideas are very different from the conclusions of B.F. Skinner.

William Barrett — *Death of the Soul: From Descartes to the Computer*. Garden City, NY: Anchor/Doubleday, 1986. Barrett defends the idea of a human soul (or self) against the mechanistic assumptions popular in our culture today. He is not defending a particular religious perspective. He is defending the idea of a non-material mind.

Franklin L. Baumer — *Modern European Thought: Continuity and Change in Ideas, 1600–1950*. New York: Macmillan, 1977. Baumer surveys five themes found in European thought. Of particular interest are those sections of the book which look at the idea of "man" from the Renaissance to the present.

Jonathan Benthall, ed.

The Limits of Human Nature. New York: E.P. Dutton, 1973. This book contains fourteen lectures by noted authorities in biology, philosophy, linguistics, and other fields.

Peter Berger, Brigitte Berger, and Hansfried Kellner

The Homeless Mind. New York: Vintage/Random House, 1973. This fairly easy to read text introduces the reader to contemporary discussions of the social construction of reality. The authors discuss how social forces shape our understanding of ourselves and our world. This line of thinking leads one to conclude that everything is relative to one's particular cultural training.

Christopher J. Berry

Human Nature. Atlantic Highlands, NJ: Humanities Press International, 1986. Berry discusses how various views of human nature play a role in political theory and practice.

Emil Brunner

Man in Revolt: A Christian Anthropology. Translated by Olive Wyon. Philadelphia: Westminster Press, 1939. This is an in-depth study of human nature from a Christian perspective.

Thomas D. Davis

Philosophy: An Introduction Through Original Fiction, Discussion, and Readings. New York: McGraw-Hill, 1993. This is a fun, and a little weird, collection of short stories with philosophical themes. The first two stories deal with freedom and determinism. Other stories deal with ethics, reality, and the nature of the mind.

Carl N. Degler

In Search of Human Nature: The Decline and Revival of Darwinism in American Social Thought. New York: Oxford, 1991. Degler explains in a historical format how Darwinism has influenced social scientists' understanding of human nature over the last one hundred twenty years.

Viktor E. Frankl

Man's Search for Meaning. New York: Pocket Books, 1957. Frankl is a psychiatrist who survived Hitler's death camps. From his own experiences and the experiences of others, Frankl developed a view of human nature and psychotherapy. He writes that a fundamental part of every human is a longing for meaning and purpose in their lives.

Erich Fromm	*Marx's Concept of Man.* New York: Frederick Ungar, 1966. This is a collection of Karl Marx's earlier writings about human nature. Fromm provides commentary and introduction. Although Marx's ideas are no longer a dominant force in today's political world, his ideas still influence people in other fields.
Erich Fromm and Ramon Xirau	*The Nature of Man.* New York: Macmillan, 1968. This is a collection of seventy-two brief statements about human nature. The selections begin with ancient religious writings and end with twentieth-century authors. The emphasis is on philosophy in this collection.
M.R. Haight	*A Study of Self-Deception.* Atlantic Highlands, NJ: Humanities Press, 1980. If humans are a single operating system, how could that system deceive itself? If self deception is possible, are there two or more parts of our selves which are seeking to dominate each other? This book opens an interesting area of study about human nature.
Anthony A. Hoekema	*Created in God's Image.* Grand Rapids, MI: Eerdmans, 1986. This is a theological and historical study of the biblical concept of "in God's image." What does the Bible mean when it says that humans are created in the image of God? How have theologians understood this term for the past two thousand years?
Aldous Huxley	*Brave New World.* New York: Harper and Row, 1932. This thought provoking novel looks into a possible future when humans are genetically prepared from conception for particular roles in an extremely planned society. This novel should be read and compared to B.F. Skinner's *Walden Two*, Arthur Koestler's *Darkness at Noon*, and George Orwell's *1984*.
Arthur Koestler	*The Ghost in the Machine.* New York: Random House, 1967. Koestler believes that biological evolution has created in human nature a complex and contradictory set of responses. He concludes that humans are both creative and destructive, rational and irrational.
Michael Landmann	*Philosophical Anthropology.* Philadelphia: Westminster Press, 1974. A historical survey of views of human nature with commentary from an

existential perspective. Landmann does a good job of exposing the assumptions which guide various viewpoints.

C.S. Lewis — *The Abolition of Man*. New York: Macmillan, 1947. This book defends the idea that human nature contains a moral element. Despite what relativists have said about morals in this century, Lewis believes that all humans share a common moral awareness.

Arthur O. Lovejoy — *The Great Chain of Being*. Cambridge, MA: Harvard University Press, 1936. Lovejoy shows that throughout Western history, many thinkers have believed that humans occupy a special place in God's creation. Humans are understood to be higher than the animals, but lower than the angels.

Robert W. Lundin — *Theories and Systems of Psychology*. Second Edition. Lexington, MA: D.C. Heath, 1979. This textbook gives a survey of the history of psychology. Lundin dedicates chapters to various schools of thought within this discipline. This book, and others like it, can give one greater perspective and understanding when reading particular psychologists.

Julian Offray de la Mettrie — *Man a Machine*. La Salle, IL: Open Court, 1912. (Original French edition, 1748.) This is an interesting discussion of how humans can be understood in purely mechanical terms, written by a physician two hundred fifty years ago.

Michel de Montaigne — *In Defense of Raymond Sebond*. 1580. This playful, sarcastic work presents a picture of humanity which is weak, but arrogant; ignorant, but proud; and confused, but confident that it has the truth.

Reinhold Niebuhr — *The Nature and Destiny of Man*. New York: Charles Scribner's Sons, 1943. Niebuhr presents a neo-orthodox, Protestant view of human nature, while also looking at opposing views of human nature in the twentieth century.

John R. Platt, ed. — *New Views of the Nature of Man*. Chicago: University of Chicago Press, 1965. This is a collection of lectures by various scientists on the issue of human nature.

Karl R. Popper and John C. Eccles	*The Self and Its Brain.* New York: Springer-Verlag, 1981. This work is detailed, interesting, and difficult. The highly respected authors (one is a neurobiologist and one is a philosopher) discuss the complexity of the human consciousness. Though many features of our lives have mechanical roots in the brain, the authors also acknowledge features which are more than mere biology.
Philip H. Rhinelander	*Is Man Incomprehensible to Man?* Stanford, CA: Stanford Alumni Association, 1973. This work defends the complexity and mystery of human nature. The author does not have a specific view of human nature.
Paul Roubiczek	*The Misinterpretation of Man: Studies in European Thought of the Nineteenth Century.* Port Washington, NY: Kennikat Press, 1947. This survey of nineteenth century thought focuses on assumptions held about human nature. This work is helpful because the ideas of the nineteenth century often continued into the twentieth century.
Leslie Stevenson	*Seven Theories of Human Nature.* Second Edition. New York: Oxford Press, 1987. Stevenson gives a commentary on seven approaches to human nature which have influenced our civilization: Plato, Christianity, Marx, Freud, Sartre, Skinner, and Lorenz.
Leslie Stevenson, ed.	*The Study of Human Nature: Readings.* New York: Oxford Press, 1981. This is a collection of important writings about human nature from ancient times to the present.
Paul Tournier	*The Meaning of Persons.* New York: Harper and Row, 1957. Tournier attempts to understand human nature by weaving together the insights of Freud and Jung, the discoveries of biology and medicine, and the ideas of philosophy and Christianity.
Mary Stewart Van Leeuwen	*The Person in Psychology: A Contemporary Christian Appraisal.* Grand Rapids, MI: Eerdmans, 1985. Van Leeuwen is a psychologist who examines her field from both philosophical and Christian perspectives. She also gives brief surveys

of the history of psychology from ancient to post-modern thought.

Chad Walsh

From Utopia to Nightmare. New York: Harper and Row, 1962. The theme of a perfectly planned community has intrigued authors and readers for centuries. Walsh examines the issues surrounding the idea of utopia and recent literary works (such as 1984) which are called "dystopias." The issue of what is constant within human nature and what is formed by social conditions is central to all discussions of utopia.

Simone Weil

The Need for Roots. Translated by Arthur Wills. New York: Harper and Row, 1952. The first part of Weil's book is an interesting exploration into the basic social, emotional, and ethical needs of all humans. She does not directly discuss human nature; she is looking at the common needs of all people.

Don M. Wolfe

The Image of Man in America. Second Edition. New York: Thomas Y. Crowell, 1970. This commentary quickly surveys ideas of human nature in American thought.

INDEX